RAIS

PROJECT

FINANCE

Handbook

and

Official

User Guide

Other books by the same author:
ALTERNATIVE CAPITAL RAISING: Business Funding in the New
Capital Markets (2011)

THE BRETTON WOODS LEGACY: Thriller novel available on Amazon.
(2021)

CONTENTS

Foreword   4

Chapter 1:   History and Introduction   10

Chapter 2:   Welcome to the Maze   28

Chapter 3:   What is 'Shovel Ready'?   42

Chapter 4:   The Project Plan (PP)   56

Chapter 5:   The Executive Summary (ES)   83

Chapter 6:   Financing Structures

Chapter 7:   Financier Types and How to Find Them   97

Chapter 8:   Fifteen Ways to Lose Your Funder   109

Chapter 9:   Engagement and Protocols   130

Chapter 10:   Arbitrage Trading   141

Chapter 11:   The Project Finance Exchange (PFX) Introduction   147

Glossary   173

FOREWORD

+

I t is a little known fact among business leaders that project finance is available in abundance, and that *genuine* project finance leaves the project principals carrying no financial liability whatsoever. Simply put, project financiers secure and underwrite their financing against the track record and financial stability of whoever is going to buy the output from the project (energy, hotel, clinics/hospitals, transport etc) and the same criteria on whoever is going to build it. These are the EPC (Engineering, Procurement and Construction) and other contractors involved in the build.

But project finance has its own way of doing things. Over recent decades there have been countless books published on project finance modelling, techniques and structures and the intricacies of infrastructure, renewables, resorts/hotels and countless other sectors.

But, amongst all those books there has not been a single one that provides guidance on where and how to find a funder, the pitfalls for the unwary, what steps to take to ensure the submission is taken seriously or why the executive summary can spell success or failure for your application. Or how to know when a project is genuinely 'shovel ready' and fit for submission, who it should be submitted to or, critically, how to submit it.

There has been no book that explains the demarcation between project financing from institutional and private capital sources, or how to spot and avoid 'joker-brokers', so your project is not shopped all over the market and becomes valueless.   Or a book that provides a backgrounder to how the market has evolved, and how best to fit yourself into it.

There has been no book that defines the different 'financier types' what their financing criteria are, or how to find them.

Or, crucially, how to ensure that when the project is actually submitted to a genuine funder, they are assured from the start that the greatest sin of all, wasting their time, is not about to be committed.

Fragmented

Few of those starting out on their project finance journey realise that they are entering a fragmented and frustrating market with their funding sources ranging across investment banks; asset managers; hedge funds; private equity & debt funds; single- and multi-family offices; private banks; wealth managers; private investment managers and a whole lexicon of other entities all carrying out the same basic function. Which is to channel $trillions of private capital into what is regarded as a safe, long term private debt and/or equity investment: *project finance*.

Every one of those entities, tens of thousands of them across the world, are all working to their own mandates and structures. Meaning there are probably almost as many different financing structures as there are channels. But no matter what the structure, the information requirements around which each one is built are common to all.

The RAISING PROJECT FINANCE Handbook guides the reader along the path to preparing their submission so that it will be acceptable to *all* financiers across *all* channels.

But while those raising the capital have their own challenges, it is not all plain sailing for investors either. Those responsible for sourcing the opportunities, or deal origination, find themselves operating in the same fragmented market, meaning those deals that they do manage to identify are not necessarily the best for them or their investors.

There are thousands of projects in all parts of the world on the sell-side and thousands of prospective financiers on the buy-side which is challenge enough for any market. Add to the individual and unique requirements of those thousands of projects and financiers. To say that this is a 'fragmented' market would be an understatement.

This is the key inhibitor on a market with the potential to release $trillions of finance into projects worldwide.

PFX NOTE: A small group of financiers and intermediaries have addressed this 'fragmentation' issue by developing the Project Finance Exchange (PFX).

Whilst PFX exploits fintech to maximum effect, it will never completely replace the human element with regard to quality control and the interface between projects and financiers.

As with anything, it is essential to understand the history. Therefore, the first ten chapters of this book presents how the market has grown to evolved over the decades from the mid-1960's to the first years of the 21st century. All the aspects are covered including the production of project plans and executive summaries, the understanding of being 'shovel ready', financing structures, engagement and protocols when dealing with financiers are all still totally relevant today.

Not least the essential understanding of the different types of financiers that have now, to all intents and purposes, completely replaced the role of traditional banks in the market. Financier types that now include asset managers, single- and multi-family offices, hedge funds, private debt & equity funds, private capital funds, wealth managers and private banks (many of which are now also wealth managers), mandated and corporate lenders, syndicate managers and countless other entities all working to the same end: to release trillions of dollars of private capital into projects that can deliver a stable, secure and long term return for their investors.

Ch: 11 presents how PFX works and how all those attributes described before that are still vitally important, and how they have been incorporated into the development and operation of the system.

At the end of this book:

- Finance raisers will have a full and complete understanding of how the market has evolved and developed to the point where PFX is not an option but a necessity.
- Financiers of all types will have a new appreciation of the work involved in producing an acceptable submission before it gets to them.
- Intermediaries will see the new and critical role they can now play in the ongoing development and growth of what will now become a structured 'market', deserving of the name.

CHAPTER 1:

HISTORY AND INTRODUCTION

+

I t is important to emphasise at the outset that *The RAISING PROJECT FINANCE Handbook* is not a technical publication.

It has been written for those just setting out on their project finance raising journey and, experience shows, overwhelmingly with little understanding of what exactly it is that a project financier's intake manager, analyst or deal origination executive, looks for in a submission.

The author's own experience covers more than 40 years in capital raising, from SME's in the 1980's to the latter 30 in project finance (as an intermediary and direct financier). A fragmented and frustrating market, across all sectors, which has prompted the writing of this book.

Apologies in advance to the purists, but this Handbook is for those who might have all the relevant technical skills necessary for a successful project, but little idea of the evolution and workings of the project finance 'market' as such. And no understanding at all of what investors seek in an application for finance.

So first, to understand the back story and how we all got here...

A Little History

There was a time when the inconspicuous gentleman on the 7.50 from somewhere in the suburbs, whose wife described his job as 'something in the City', was master of the universe. He was often adorned with a bowler hat and read the *FT, Times* or *Telegraph* to pass the time on his commute.

At the end of the day he got the 5.17 home, where his family would be waiting for him at the dinner table.

As the world turned this ritual was repeated in the financial centres across Europe, the USA and, such as they were at the time, Asia ...probably without the bowler hat.

These were the people who had controlled the money from the very inception of the banking and financial markets through to the mid-1960's. They worked for banks and other financial institutions, many of which have long since disappeared, who had the access to capital and the final say on where and how it could be spent.

Capital was at the beck and call of those who already had it. If you were a huge corporation and you wanted to build a factory, bridge or hotel in another country or any other project you would go to your bank and, through their networks channels, capital would become available to you.

This usually happened in the form of syndicated loans and similar structures. Remember the 'tombstones' that used to appear in the financial media? All those financial institutions that would line up behind a lead underwriter to put their own and their client's money into a company that everyone had heard of? For any kind of early-stage or mid-market operation in any sector, access to 'project size' finance was not even on the radar.

Sometimes, a company could find the wherewithall to fund a 'flotation' (now an IPO – Initial Public Offering) on their stock exchange. Not a cheap undertaking, even now.

But the participants would be the lead bank (or merchant bank back in the day) and a close circle of their peers and financial institutions such as pension, insurance, mutual and fixed income funds, with Joe Public excluded from the action. What would he know anyway?

But, from the late-1960's things began to change when the Eurodollar bond market appeared and, by the mid-1970's had manifested itself as the world's largest capital market. Ever. It channelled ex-pat U.S. dollars into loans for governments and major corporations all over the world.

Billions upon billions of dollars that had been generated outside of the U.S., and stayed there because of the taxation they would have been hit with back home, found their way through the Eurobond market into every corner of the world.

The dividends (coupons) this market generated remained outside of the U.S., channelled into multiple domiciles through the investment banks that came to dominate the market.

It has been argued that the Eurodollar bond market was the genesis of the global capital markets as we know them today.

Egalitarian

From here, slowly but surely, the investment banks started to encroach on the *status quo* until, by the late-1970's a bowler hat had become a rare sight indeed.

A new breed of banker... ambitious, impatient and aggressive was ruling the roost.

To the point where, by the early 1980's regulations had fallen far behind what was happening in the real world. Technology, too, was a new force propelling ever developing and evolving markets in which, it seemed, anybody could play, in new and unpredictable directions.

The beginning of the end was when traditional retail banks, in an effort to keep up with developments acquired, merged with or set up their own investment banks. It was plain to see (without calling on hindsight) what was coming as, fatally, there were no discernible borders between their conflicting risk-inclined and risk-averse (investment and retail respectively) cultures. We all know what happened then.

It took a while but, eventually, the regulators caught up and that particular debacle was dealt with. Out of all that came a more egalitarian market place. In the 1990's business angels and venture capital (VC) made their first appearance. Funds were set up that could direct capital from private individuals and companies into smaller or mid-market enterprises.

The first small-cap markets like London's AIM began to appear. Things were changing, and mostly for the better.

Then came private equity (PE) funds driven by people who came out of the investment banking culture. Someone had worked out that you could take a growing company, put in some private money (equity) and then leverage that money, along with the track record and prospects of the company, into loan capital.

Hey presto! A formula that could deliver new money into growing, mid-market companies, without the need for a float/IPO or all that loan syndication bother. Except that the loans were often over-leveraged to the point where the companies themselves would buckle under the load.

But there was another kind of PE fund overlooked by the financial media which, to a large extent, was working in tandem with VC's. Private individuals could put their money into these funds and leave it to the experts to place it into SME, mid-tier or even large companies or, indeed, anything that could show an acceptable EBITDA, along with equally acceptable risk for their investors.

This is still an unregulated market where institutional capital, ie: that from pension, fixed income and similar regulated funds cannot tread. For them, anything they invest in, usually debt, has to show an acceptable credit agency (Moody's, S&P or Fitch) rating. More on this later (*Chapter 6: Financing Structures*) but, for now, PE funds were filling a big need using private capital from risk-inclined investors.

Then hedge funds appeared, to a large extent an offshoot of PE. Bigger, better managed often with people from the more enlightened end of the investment banking spectrum, they became a powerful force in the market by the turn of the century.

Indeed, since the arrival of hedge funds, investment banks as such are few and far between.

But even hedge funds are now being challenged since the wealthy individuals that provide their capital have taken to managing their own investments through the new kid on the block, their family offices. In July 2019 Campden Wealth, one of the leading groups in the market, said there are "...7,300 single family offices worldwide, up a significant 38% from 2017.

The largest proportion of those 7,300 family offices were based in North America (42% or 3,100), followed by Europe (32% or 2,300 offices), Asia Pacific (18% or 1,300 offices), and the emerging markets of South America, Africa and the Middle East (8% or 600 offices). This development is the manifestation of the tectonic upheavals that have been progressively destabilising the traditional capital markets since the 1990's."

When you have 90% of the world's wealth now owned by .02 of its population (depending on whose data you believe) something has to give.

Dry Powder
It is hard to say when the term 'project finance' first made an appearance, although the first recorded project financ*ing* was in 1299 by an Italian merchant bank, the House of Frescapaldi, funding English silver mines, with the loan repaid with the output from the mines. Which, in itself, is the very definition of 'project finance'.

The data presented in this book may, in time, become a little dated, but links are provided so that readers can catch up with current numbers.

But fast forward seven centuries from 1299 and it is safe to say that the structure has been significantly refined. There was a major re-set in the 1950's, which became the basis for the structure as we know it now. But, even from then it is unrecognisable. With the more recent advent of A+-rated insurance wraps, backed by Lloyds-of-London and other leading insurance markets, and with transactions now being conducted through SPV's, today's project finance structure is genuinely 'non-recourse'. But where does the money come from now?

For sure, it is no longer the man in the bowler hat. In 2018 McKinsey estimated that hedge funds were sitting on $1.8tn of funds looking for something to do, otherwise known as 'dry powder'. In February 2019 EY published a survey showing that fundraising for private credit vehicles stood at US$110.2bn across 157 separate vehicles in 2018 alone. Although this was down 12% from 2017, the appetite for fundraising remained strong, with almost 400 private credit vehicles raising more than US$168bn in aggregate at that time.

The Insurance Wrapped Project Finance (IWPF) program, which is separated from the crowd by its ability to 'credit enhance' suitable projects with a credit agency 'A' rating, has an annual facility of $300bn (at the time of writing) from the institutional capital markets. Thus releasing normally risk-averse institutional capital into the previously 'unrated' project finance market.

IWPF has since evolved into a project finance Wrap product which is now being applied to many projects, principally through PFX.

But Family Offices, which first made an appearance around 2005, and already mentioned above, no doubt existed before then, but were very private and had not actually been endowed with a name as such. These are the private offices of Ultra High Net Worth Individuals (UHNWI's), ie: billionaires, along with those thousands of multi-millionaires bordering on that status.

The Economist reported that, at a conference for UHNWI's and their family offices in Dubai in December 2018, there was over $2tn in the room.

The 2020 Cap-Gemini World Wealth Report, the longest running survey in the 'wealth industry' gave a population of 19.6 HNWI's with their wealth increased by 8.8% and 8.6% respectively in 2019, significantly higher than the 2018 decline rates of 0.3% and 2.9%.

The Cap-Gemini definition of a HNWI is anyone with liquid cash of one million dollars or more over all other assets including house, cars, boat etc. Their total worth in 2019 was put at $74 trillion.

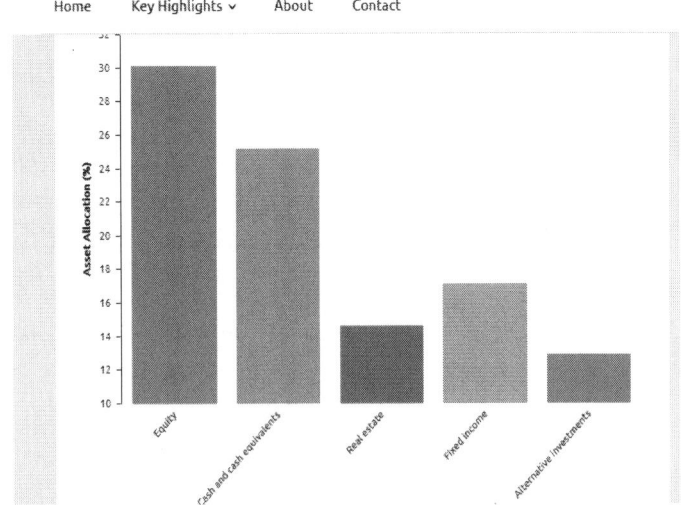

But it was the Asset Allocation bar chart (above) in the report which is of the most interest to those involved in the global project finance market.

We can set aside the 30% allocated to equity as this will be for the public capital markets, which provides the liquidity that U/HNWI's need   To get a feel for what proportion of all this private wealth goes to project finance we need to look at real estate (14%) and alternative investments (13%).

A total of 27% of $74tn of private capital equating to $19.98tn.   Even if just ten percent of this sum finds its way into projects, which deliver the long-term return which financiers seek, that still equates to c$2tn of finance available to the global project finance market.

However, we know that there is significantly more of this 'dry powder' waiting to be deployed wherever it can generate a reasonably safe and worthwhile return for all these U/HNWI's.

Are there funds available for my project?

 There is abundant capital available. It is simply a matter of bringing structure and purpose to your quest for your share of it. The only time it is worth paying for anyone's help in the task when they can prove they have direct access to funders and can enhance, or 'professionalise' your submission.

The upshot is that, after decades of evolution, the actual font of all the wealth is now doing it for itself. The source of the funds, U/HNWI's and their family offices, are now seeking to originate and structure their own deals. In many ways the larger of these Family Offices have become, and behave, just like what can be regarded in the market as Asset Managers or Hedge Funds.

So, even in these few short paragraphs we have exposed an absolute minimum of c$2tn of dry powder (we can be sure that is not all of it) some of which could be directed into your project.

Please note the data above was assembled in 2021. Please use the links provided for further current research.

Project Finance Sources

So, from the all-powerful man in the bowler hat we have progressed to a point where the options to raise project finance are actually confusing in their diversity and numbers.

Private capital, equal to (or exceeding) institutional capital in volume, is channelled into the market through countless entities all performing, essentially, the same task. Which is directing private wealth into countless projects and enterprises.

They go under many banners such as private equity & debt funds, alternative investment funds, asset managers, private capital funds, private office, single family office, multi-family office, wealth manager and many others, including a growing number of private banks which are also wealth managers.

All these 'wealth reports' vary, but another, the Wealth-X *The World Ultra-Wealth report 2019* uses different 'qualifying' criteria and puts forward that there were 353,550 U/HNWI's with a projected total wealth of $43 trillion by 2023. Unfortunately, there are no surveys to show how much of this is invested in institutional (regulated) funds, meaning those surveys that are undertaken do not help our efforts to define accurately what money is available to what type of project financing.

However, because of the sheer numbers of the various private capital channels now operating, it has to be assumed that the estimate of $2 trillion put forward in this book is perfectly reasonable and could easily be doubled, or more.

So the upshot is that there are now two kinds of project finance available.

1. Institutional Capital

That which is available only to entities that can present a credit agency rating of 'A' or above. These are limited to major corporates, municipalities and local authorities and, sometimes, quasi-governmental entities. Money from the institutional capital markets is the cheapest available because, being regulated (because they are 'retail', ie: managing money on behalf of pensioners, policy-holders etc), they can lend only to entities with minimal 'A' or better risk, meaning low interest.

But access to it is limited to those who can show the necessary Moody's, S&P or Fitch rating.

Institutional capital can be defined as that provided by pension, fixed-income, mutual, insurance and similar funds all operating under their specific regulatory regimes.

For the vast majority of projects seeking finance, institutional capital is out of reach.

However, the recent introduction of A+-rated insurance 'Wraps' has made the market more attractive to institutional investors.

2. **Private Capital**

   An unregulated market where private capital is available to projects that can show all the necessary requirements of risk-mitigation to a private capital source. Meaning that whatever is going to be built has a contracted credible buyer for whatever it is going to produce, as also required by institutional capital.

   Also, that the EPC (Engineering, Procurement and Construction) contractor and all other participants and suppliers to the build and ongoing operation of the project can show financial stability and track record. Decisions can sometimes be very subjective with regard to what sectors, deal values, regions and other criteria are of the highest interest to the investor at the time.

   Where there is no contracted buyer, but revenues come from a known market such as with hotels/resorts, transport infrastructure, hospitals etc, a feasibility study from a credible source is required. Also as demanded by institutional lenders.

For the vast majority of projects, because that vast majority does not have the prerequisite credit agency 'A' rating, the only viable option is private capital.

Private project finance capital can therefore be defined as that being invested or lent by private (largely unregulated) entities (once generically referred to as 'shadow banking') to projects that do not carry a credit agency 'A' rating.

There is another significant difference between the institutional and private capital markets. Regulations themselves lend structure to the institutional markets and for municipalities, major corporations and others who can show the pre-requisite credit agency rating, long standing relationships will lead a borrower direct to the source.

These entities also often have their own corporate and project financing departments and teams qualified to produce exactly the documentation required to show to their institutional lenders and to play a large part in structuring and syndicating their own financings.

Many will have lines of credit set up with these institutions so that calling down funds, on terms that can only be dreamed of by those without the necessary credit agency rating, is merely a matter of process. They work in the hundreds of millions and, quite often, billions as a matter of course.

Contradictions

The private capital market on the other hand, is fragmented and frustrating confusion. Consequently it is riddled with contradictions and infested with dreamers, scammers and joker-brokers. Whether you are looking for start-up, development, mezzanine, M&A, venture or project finance the story is the same.

There is no single 'market place' through which buy- and sell-sides can meet. But, in this book, we are separating out and focusing exclusively on **project** finance.

Critically, and experience bears this out, there are still influential principals on some projects that regard any financier that is not a bank or other institution with a name they recognise is not worth talking to. Indeed, should be avoided.

This will change in time but, meanwhile, there are many totally viable projects that go nowhere because some principals on the project, usually an ex-banker or lawyer, simply shrug off the names they do not recognise.

Remember, banks have largely retreated from the project finance market and, for those that remain, act very much as loan syndicators or aggregators. Some offer comprehensive debt and/or equity structured finance, but not with their own money.

In summary, finding your way through this labrynthine market is your biggest challenge. The RAISING PROJECT FINANCE Handbook which is now also the Official PFX

User Guide has been written to help you through this maze.

Interestingly, in the wake of the 2008 crash, all those private institutions mentioned above, ie: family offices, hedge funds, private debt and equity funds, mandated lenders etc, came to be referred to as the 'shadow banking' sector by the global financial establishment.

Which is ironic, when it is generally considered that the so-called 'shadow banking' sector has come to clearly overshadow traditional banks. Most certainly when it comes to the $multi-trillion global project finance market.

But this is not all good news. Before 2008, there was a fixed 'go-to' point for financing of any sort, which was 'the bank'. However, project financing is, essentially, lending against revenues from a yet-to-be-built asset, from, which mainstream banks are excluded by their own regulations.

Now, with traditional banks effectively excluded from the project finance market, and many other financing sectors, project leaders are left with nowhere definitive to go.

The market is now comprised of many thousands of private capital sources, as already described above, all trying to connect with the many thousands of projects seeking finance at any one time.

We are left with a fragmented and confusing maze which, hopefully, this Handbook will help you navigate.

As time goes on the data coming from the so-called 'shadow banking' (private wealth/capital and its institutions) sector will evolve. For up-to-date information the following sources are considered by the author to be the most informative:

Campden Wealth (www.campdenwealth.com) providing intelligence to the world's wealthiest families, their family office and ultra-high net worth investors since 1987.

Credit-Suisse Global Wealth Report (use as Google search term)
A comprehensive overview of trends in Ultra High Net Worth data.

EMPEA (Emerging Markets Private Equity Association) (www.empea.org)
The global industry association for private capital in emerging markets.
Global Project Finance Review (www.pfie.com)
Published by Thomson Reuters presents data on project finance loans across North America, Europe & Middle East Arena and other areas.

Knght Frank Wealth Report (Use as search term)
Measures the size of HNWI, UHNWI and billionaire cohorts in over 200 countries and territories.

McKinscy (www.mckinsey.com)
Their Private Capital Markets Review provides useful insight to investor types and preferences.

Pitchbook (www.pitchbook.com)
Financial data and software providing data on public and private markets.

Private Debt Investor (www.privatedebtinvestor.com)
Tracks the investment appetite of private debt investors

Preqin (www.preqin.com)
Provides data from c100,000 private capital market participants covering family offices, all private financing sources as well as consultants and advisors active in the market.

Wealth-X (www.wealthx.com)
Lifestyle focus on the very wealthy supported with regular data updates

Global Wealth Report 2023 | UBS Global
UBS has now taken the lead in maintaining the watch on global wealth. The link above will take you to their 2023 Exec Summary.

The panel below presents the distribution of 'dry powder' across the various types of private capital fund:

Global Private Capital Market
Key Data

Fund Type	AUM
2,000 Alternative Investment Funds	$ 2tn[1]
10,000 Hedge funds	$ 3.2tn[2]
7,300 Multi-/Single-Family Offices	$ 5.9tn[3]
62,000 Private debt and equity funds	$ 5.5tn[4]
45,000 Asset Mgrs (IAM membership)	$10tn*

Estimate taken from combined physical and liquid assets of $100tn as presented by Thinking Ahead Institute. IAM membership does not represent all Asset Mgrs.

Total Funds/AUM: **126,000/$26.6tn**

*Total AUM of $26.6tn broadly reflects Cap-Gemini's of total $24tn available to alternative assets and RE.

Private Capital Source

19 million U/HNWI's

Aggregate wealth $74tn[5]

[1] AIMA
[2] Hedge Fund Assoc
[2] eVestment
[3] Campden Wealth
[4] Pensions & Investments Mag
[4] Preqin
[4] Pitchbook
[5] Asset Allocation chart. Cap-Gemini World Wealth Report.

Chapter 2:

Welcome to the Maze

+

n my previous book (2011) co-authored with Ariane Richter and now long overtaken by events, *Alternative Capital Raising in the New Capital Markets,* there was a chapter titled: *Scams, Mills and Joker-Brokers*.

At the time, just three years after the crash of 2008 the market was awash with thousands of redundant bankers. Each of them convinced that they had the connections to offer up not just project but all kinds of other financing to every kind of capital raising entity.

Few, if any, actually did and most have now found themselves safe berths again somewhere back in the banking and finance industry, or moved onto other things.

For a time, possibly up until 2014 or 2015, this over-population of 'brokers' and 'advisors' continued to pollute the market but, in more recent times, the fog seems to have cleared. But what we are now seeing is professionals including qualified financial advisors of various disciplines, lawyers and others putting themselves forward as project finance advisors.

Experience shows that a good proportion of them have no idea about the submission or funding process, or even what separates 'project' from other forms of finance. But because they come with professional qualifications, it lends credibility to their presentation.

It is important to emphasise that this is most certainly *not* the case with all of them, those that have actual experience and funder connections in the market will be able to make that very clear. Those that have not will try to mask it through highly professional and polished presentation.

The documentation they produce including their NDA's and fee agreements is of the highest standard and sufficient to impress anyone who is just starting out on their project financing journey. But there is just one problem, while the NDA is fine they would not need a fee agreement with you if they were a gatekeeper who is direct to project financiers. They should have their own fee agreement direct with those financiers.

Financiers that are happy to work with introducers or intermediaries, otherwise known as gatekeepers, are happy to pay an introduction fee to them directly concurrent with releasing funds to the client.

Genuine gatekeepers and other intermediaries know, usually through hard-won experience, that there are no fast bucks to be made as a project finance intermediary. And it can take many years to build a reputation and trust with genuine financiers.

The challenge for those setting out to raise project finance is to discern between those who know what they are doing, and those who only *think* they do. But by far the best way to get your project in front of a *genuine* financier is to seek out a *genuine* project finance intermediary or gatekeeper.

In a fragmented and unstructured market, populated by thousands on both the buy and sell sides at any one time, these are the people who know their way around, much like a mortgage broker.

Joker-broker chains

It is essential to be so very, very careful. There is no problem in paying a lawyer, project finance advisor or other professional to assist you in the production of your project plan and assembling all the necessary documentation or, if they are able, make an introduction to a financier. If they actually know what they are doing, that is par for the course.

But if you see a fee that has to be paid on completion, be it one percent or five percent of principal, take care. Because it is not you who is going to pay this fee, it is the financier.

And no financier is going to be railroaded into paying anyone's fee if they had no hand in agreeing it. It can be a deal-breaker.

How do I know I'm dealing with a genuine intermediary or gatekeeper?

If there is a completion fee in your Engagement Agreement check that their funder has agreed to pay that fee on completion. This will produce a straight 'yes' or 'no' answer'.

Or maybe a deafening silence.

You are in danger of walking into the dreaded 'broker chain' where your deal is passed between an endless array of 'brokers' who have no idea of where your money is going to come from, but still want a slice of it if and when it appears.

These are the ones who believe that life changing amounts of money will come their way simply by forwarding your project onto their contacts or, even worse, turning it into e-mail spam.

Broker chains are a deal killer.

Not only is your deal absorbed into an unfathomable maze of dreamers and time-wasters, it will be 'shopped' around the market to the point where, once a genuine funder does get to hear about it, they will not be inclined to follow through with it.

Also, that old chestnut about the 'reading fee', *ie*: paying someone a fee of anywhere between $2,500 and $10,000 simply to review your submission, has gone the way of all scams. Eventually, people see the light.

The only 'upfront' fee you should expect to pay is if your advisor is providing assistance on preparing your submission in the form of a detailed, submission ready, project plan.

It's Not Who You Know

But, out of all the failings of project principals, where hope doesn't just spring eternal, it often sets aside reality, is that there is an over-reliance on people they already know.

If you are a team of people, fully qualified in your respective professional disciplines and well on the way to having your project plan ready for submission, what are the chances that any one of you is going to be directly connected to a funder, or a gatekeeper to a genuine funder?

If you are talking to your own accountant, financial advisor or any other party assisting you with your project who tells you that they can help with funding, ask yourself the simple question: *"Out of all the people I know are any of them a project financier, or gatekeeper to a project financier who would be interested in my project?"*

The numbers dictate that the answer must, overwhelmingly, be 'no'. But, if you pursue your project financing through someone you know you will, in the majority of cases, be led into the weird and twilight world of the joker-broker.

No matter how well you know them, even if they are close friends, ask for proof of project financings they have been involved with before, and to suggest a possible funder. If they cannot do that, start your search from scratch.

Google 'project finance advisors [your city, state, country, region etc]' or, add 'renewable energy', 'hotel/resort' or any other sector to the search. Look at their website bearing in mind the bigger and better produced the website does not necessarily mean they are actually the best for you.

Some of the biggest and most active financiers in the market have no website at all and work exclusively through their networks of trusted intermediaries and gatekeepers, simply to keep the chaos that prevails across the market at arm's length. Further information on this in *Chapter 7: Financier Types and How to Find Them.*

You can also try 'direct project financing', but you will not find much. Genuine project financiers keep quite a low profile so that they are not spending all their time filtering out the dross, and prefer to work with trusted gate-keepers who risk *their* time performing that task (in return for their completion/introduction fee.

There are some notable exceptions to this rule, who have the in-house analysts and intake managers to do what gate-keepers normally do. But even they will also work with trusted gate-keepers.

The upshot of your search should be a selection of gatekeepers (because actual funders keep such a low profile) that you can talk to.

Prepare a short, sharp summary, an elevator pitch, not necessarily a full executive summary (as in *Chapter 5: The. Executive Summary and Submission*) and explain that you are now preparing your project for submission. Send this to all of them and set up a call

Questions you should ask are:

- **Have you been involved in the completion of any project finance transactions?**
  Don't ask who, where or how much as the NDA's they have signed will prevent them from telling you. An answer 'yes' with an indication of deal sectors, locations and values should suffice.

- **What are your completion fee arrangements? Does the investor pay you, or do you expect us to pay?**

  The preferred answer is that the funder pays them directly. If they say that they will have a fee agreement with you the chances are that they are not direct to the funder.

- **If they expect you to pay, ask: Does the investor agree that we pay this fee to you and are they happy to fund this fee?**

  This will clarify if you are dealing with a joker-broker or someone who knows what they are doing – a seasoned intermediary or gatekeeper.

- **Are you direct to the financier or are you the investor?**

  Sometimes (rarely) a good project finance advisor or gatekeeper is actually contracted into the funding consortium making them 'the investor'. This is the ideal situation. But 'we are direct to the funder' is equally positive.

- **Where is your investor located?**

  Do not be put off if the answer is somewhere far removed from where you are, maybe on the other side of the planet. Project finance is a global market with most funders willing to lend/invest in any politically stable country or region.

- **What fees do you charge?**

  These should be limited to fees charged to assist in the preparation of your documentation, if you ask for it, and ensuring that you have secured all the necessary permits, permissions, contracts and agreements so you are at a genuinely 'submission ready' stage when you submit. Read on to see why you will never be 'shovel ready' when you submit your project for financing.

  If this is your first project financing transaction it is worthwhile paying the intermediary to assist in assembling and/or producing all your submission documentation. Anything along the lines of reading fee, intake fee or any other fee, hang up.

- **Can you assure me that my project is not going to be passed onto any other brokers or intermediaries?**

  While the answer to this is preferably 'yes', over the past few years there has been a 'Tier-1' intermediary/gate-keeper network evolving within which deals are passed between them and resulting fees shared. Many of these were instrumental in setting up the Project Finance Exchange (PFX). If this is going to be the case with your transaction, ensure that the necessary NDA's are in place and demand that you are kept advised of who has seen your deal.

Your gatekeeper must be no more than one part removed from the funding source.

If you are completely satisfied with the answers you are getting ask for the engagement agreement (which will preferably not show a completion fee) and NCNDA.

Project Finance Initiation (PFI) costs

There are some project principals who expect to go all the way through to full project financing without spending a single dollar, pound, euro or any contribution at all to getting the job done.

These are the dreamers, and financiers and gate-keepers do all we can to avoid them.

Your author along with many others has an intake form in which we ask basic questions like: Do you have all necessary permits and permissions?; Do you own the land?; Are all contracts and agreements (EPC, feedstock provider, off-take etc) in place? To which we hope to get the answers 'yes'. All these things incur cost to some degree and to say, effectively, that this money has been spent, when it has not, which happens more times than you can imagine, is simply a waste of everybody's time. And word will quickly get around.

The 'dreamers' can sometimes have brilliant ideas and, quite often, go some way towards realising them by talking to all the right people, but you have to walk the talk as well.

It takes hard cash to secure your environmental, construction, wayleave and other permits. It costs hard cash in legal fees for your EPC or off-taker to produce their agreements and contracts, to which you could well be expected to contribute. These are the Project Finance Initiation (PFI) costs.

PFI costs often bring viable projects to a premature halt for the simple reason that those who have the ideas, often do not have the financial wherewithall to take them to the next stage, full project financing. Perhaps there is a need for a PFI fund or network that can direct this money, mostly running to between $100,000 and $500,000 (sometimes less, sometimes more depending on the size and type of project) into these opportunities.

Such a fund could very easily invest these sums for significant equity stakes of anywhere between 10% and 40%+ in projects with values running into the $100's of millions or $billions with EBITDA's often as high as 15% or more. Depending on the financing structure attracted to your project, you should expect to be paying further transaction fees (over and above PFI costs) covering legal, due diligence, closing and other costs, known collectively as 'closing costs'.

These costs can go anywhere between $100,000 (sometimes less) and $500,000 (sometimes more) depending entirely on the financier, their structure, your project and countless other considerations.

When should we start our search for project finance?

The time to start looking for your financing is at the same time as you feel confident that you are going to move forward with your project and bring it to submission ready stage (see *Chapter 3: What is Submission Ready?*).

This could be a year away, but start your project financing search now, at least as far as identifying prospective financiers.

You need to have this clear between you and the investor at the outset of your discussions, so it does not come as a surprise when you start the closing process. Even better, the financier should make it clear before you even ask.

However, it is absolutely essential that you conduct your own due diligence on the financier if you have any doubts in your mind. There are *still* scams out there.

So, having got these basics all tee'd up, you need to get your project to the point where it can genuinely be called 'submission ready'. Many are the times an executive summary has been opened and, somewhere in the first two pages the bold statement is made: '*This is a shovel ready project*'.

This is the most eye-roll inducing statement you could possibly make, unless you have read the next chapter...

PFX NOTE

When you submit your project to PFX it is first scrutinized by our central team to ensure that it meets our stringent *'submission* ready' standards. It is important to keep in mind that only the investor and their counterparties (surveyors, market specialists, underwriters etc) can declare a project to be 'shovel ready'.

Once it has been assessed, quite likely involving a phone call with you, it will then be allocated to a PFX Regional Manager (RM) based on your deal value, market sector, location and other factors.

Across PFX central intake and RM's operating through 20 regional Intake Centres there is over 400 years of project finance experience working on your behalf.

CHAPTER 3:

WHAT IS 'SHOVEL READY'?

+

A fter months of planning and preparation, your cursor hovers over the 'send' button. A deep intake of breath and, maybe, a quiet prayer.

You click.

And now your project's executive summary and covering e-mail is winging its way to your prospective investor.

Of course, you will have all your supporting documentation neatly organised on Dropbox or in your data room for your funder to review, and to show that you are completely 'shovel ready'. Really?

Sorry to burst any bubbles at such a sensitive time but it is probably true to say that at least 99% of projects declaring themselves to be 'shovel ready', simply are not. Many are so far removed from that euphoric state that the submission will be consigned to the recycle bin.

For what it's worth, your author has never been presented with one, single 'shovel ready' submission in three decades of working in the market.

The rare exceptions to this rule are those that come from Tier-1 project principals such as major construction and infrastructure companies, and the global accountants/consultancies across all sectors. Ie: those who have done it all before, and who do not really need to be reading this book.

These are usually major hotels/resorts, hospitals, airports etc and, of course, public infrastructure works, submitted by government departments will usually be prepared to full and proper 'shovel ready' status. Many of these go direct to institutional lenders.

But those projects that find their way into the private capital end of the market, the overwhelming majority, are the ones that all financiers keep a special eye out for.

Even so, your author's experience shows that even these can often descend into frustrating delays through misrepresentations, no matter how small, about off-take and other agreements being available when, actually, they are not.

The overwhelming majority of submissions come from companies, teams and their SPV's where project finance is not an area of particular expertise. Or with preconceptions that are far removed from the reality. These are the ones that fall far short of being 'shovel ready' when they are first submitted.

But, in the vast majority of cases, the project has been put together by people who are really good at their jobs be it engineering, construction, renewable or O&G energy and, even, the indispensable financial management and control.

They may well have assembled a project that is fundamentally sound, but without any real knowledge of how project financing actually works. In these cases it is the funder's call as to whether or not to take the risk and invest the time necessary to pursue the transaction based on the incomplete documentation presented.

This could involve time and resources spent on educating the client as to what is needed, with no clear assurance that the transaction can be taken forward to a successful closing at the end of the day. So, what does this much abused term, 'shovel ready' actually mean?

A reasonable definition would be: A project with all construction, offtake, feedstock and other counterparty contracts signed, or ready to sign, and with all relevant permits and permissions issued and paid for.

Without all these documents assembled and presented in a format that the investor can easily review, the project is not even *submission*, let alone, shovel ready. After the investor has agreed that they are satisfied with all these documents and, of course, the financial forecasts that align with them, he will pass them to his underwriters and lawyers for further review and execution.

This will ensure the project has a proper insurance 'Wrap' and that your funding agreement is properly produced.

Only then is your project truly 'shovel ready'.

Defining a 'Project'

If you want your funder to release funds based on forecasts and market research presented in a business plan, you are asking for risk capital, which comes mostly as equity. You are talking to the wrong funder.

Am I looking for project finance, or some other form of finance?

If you are raising finance to build a factory to produce something that *market research* tells you is going to sell well into its market, you are seeking risk investment.

If, however, that factory is being built to produce something for which there is a *credible, contracted buyer*, you are seeking *project* finance.

'Project Finance' can be defined as: Financing predicated on the track record and financial stability of whoever is contracted to buy the output from the built project, and not those of the project principals.

That is project finance.

The very definition of project finance is that there is a credible someone or something contracted to buy whatever it is your project is going to produce. So, if your project is genuinely at 'submission ready' stage your documentation will include all that shown in *Chapter 4: The Project Plan (PP)*:

Prepare and organise files in Dropbox or your own data-room so they can be easily identified by your investor, their analysts, surveyors, lawyers and other third parties involved in your project financing.

Off-take agreement.

This can take many forms. In the case of an energy project, be it renewable or O&G, a credible buyer committed to taking sufficient output, a Power Purchase Agreement (PPA) to cover the terms of your financing. If a hotel project, an OMA (Operation and Management Agreement) with a credible hotel operator that will generate sufficient revenues to meet the financing terms.

The list here is endless but, no matter what the market sector or circumstances, you will need to show a contract sufficient to cover your financing terms ready to sign, or signed 'subject to financing'. Sometimes an HOA, MOU or LOI will satisfy the funder sufficiently to start work on your transaction. But no funds can be released without contracts and agreements signed on all fronts.

Naturally, your off-taker will need to show track record and financial stability to get past the underwriters.

Engineering Procurement and Construction (EPC) Contractor Agreement.

As with all your other project participants, your EPC needs to show credibility, meaning track record and financial stability. You should be able to show full costings and timelines for the entire project (integrated into your overall project .xls) with the contract covering every aspect of the undertaking. The contract can be left unsigned, or signed 'subject to financing' or, as with other project participants HOA, MOU or LOI may suffice depending on the financier.

Either way, as with all contracts on your project, they must be signed prior to release of funds.

It is impossible to emphasise enough that the funder has to know *exactly* what they are funding, every last detail of it.

Putting up your friendly neighbourhood builder to construct a $250 million resort because you go to the same church or golf club will probably not cut the mustard. Find a contractor who the funder and their underwriters will be comfortable with.

Feedstock.
Again, this can take many forms but usually it is crude for a refinery, sufficient municipal waste to feed a W2E plant or sufficient raw material for a recycling operation such as plastic for a plastics recycling plant.

One recent project declaring itself 'shovel ready' needed to show sufficient mandates from enough refineries to keep a new oil storage depot operating at optimum capacity for the entire period of the 25-year loan. There were no such mandates.

On the other side of the coin, a submission from the U.S. seeking $7bn for a major renewable energy project, and again declaring itself 'shovel ready', simply said 'the state grid will buy the energy and fuel by-products will contribute to the statutory requirements for green fuel.' Also, 'sufficient feedstock will be provided by municipalities across the state'.

Not an HOU, MOU or LOI in sight. Let alone a contract, draft or otherwise. And this submission had been approved by the state government concerned.

Your company or SPV.

Naturally, we want to know about you and your company, or the company you have formed to manage the project, the SPV (Special Purpose Vehicle). And what is a company if not its people?

Your submission will (or should) show comprehensive bio's of the personnel covering the three pillars of any successful enterprise: (i) technical/product knowledge, (ii) financial control and (iii) sales/marketing/relationships. To be sure we know exactly what it is we are financing, we need to see full signed employment contracts which, again, can be 'subject to finance'.

In your main project plan (*Chapter 4: The Project Plan*) your key personnel need to be presented in detail with professional qualifications and employment or business history in the relevant annex.

In the Executive Summary (*Chapter 5: The Executive Summary and Submission*) these details can be reduced to one or two hundred word biographies.

Feasibility studies.

In some instances it is not always possible to have the financing sharply defined with signed contracts providing the necessary underwriting comfort. An example would be transport infrastructure such as roads, bridges, ferries and the like.

In these instances it is essential to present *independent* and credible data showing that there will be traffic generating sufficient revenues to cover the financing. These are sometimes known as 'willing to pay' surveys where, if sufficient people are known to be willing to pay to use a road, bridge, ferry or similar piece of infrastructure, this will usually satisfy the financier.

If a toll road, bridge or other transport infrastructure which is going to be covered by user-revenues, evidence that traffic flows are sufficient to generate the tolls and fares necessary to cover the loan repayments.

The Surveys and Feasibility Study needs to be produced by an entity that the financier can take seriously. A respected university, regional or national transport authority, freight or other transport infrastructure user's association would be the appropriate source.

Feasibility studies are also required for real estate (RE) projects, particularly hotels and resorts, where there is no OMA. These need to be produced by an industry recognised entity such as CBRE, Savills, Colliers or the like.

This should be budgeted into your PFI (Project Finance Initiation) spend.

Permits and permissions
This can be a minefield depending on the project. Ensure that all necessary environmental, building, wayleaves and

other permits and permissions have been issued. So often we see '...will be issued on funding....' in the project plan, which simply does not work.

How can finance be released without knowing for sure that all these permits and permissions are in place? It is absolutely essential that these have all been paid for, issued, are valid and presented with your submission or, if not, an undertaken given to the financier that they will be acquired as financing structure is progressing. The financier will want confirmation from the parties concerned.

Again, these costs should be allocated to and covered in your PFI spend.

LOI, MOU, HOA etc...
In some cases, not always, it is possible to accept an LOI, MOU or HOA as sufficient to support the application. It depends very much on who is presenting the document. If it is a major EPC contractor, or a credible off-taker then most funders will start the financing process but will demand to see the final draft or signed agreement before entering closing legal stages of the agreement.

The underwriters and lawyers are going to want to see everything wrapped up tight and no LOI, MOU, HOA or similar should cross their desks once you get to closing stage.

No matter what you submit, the financier is always going to ask to see full and final contracts which, under any circumstances, will need to be signed *prior to* the release of funds – because (here we go again…) the funder needs to know *exactly* what they are financing. So it is far better to have your project participants get to final contract stage prior to submitting your application if at all possible.

This will make an instant positive impression on your financier and move your financing forward much quicker. If there are reservations on this from any of your project participants simply tell them that your funder needs to see these contracts and agreements before they can assess your project and move to underwriting stage.

On some larger projects, LOI's, MOU's and HOA's will suffice to get an agreement to fund in *principle* or a conditional terms sheet. But, no matter what, those detailed signed contracts are going to need to be on file with the funder before funds can be released.

Shovel ready, or not?
As already explained, no you are not. But you might be close to *submission* ready. Is there nothing left to chance where the funder is going to ask 'Can we see so-and-so agreement please?' or '…where's the data?' Probably not, because every project has its own unique circumstances and characteristics.

Review your submission three, four or more times before clicking that 'send' button. It's a bit like an author preparing a book for submission to their editor. They will review, re-work and polish it 20 or 30 times before they feel confident enough to send it off.

Financials

Whole books have been written, courses and seminars produced and reams of online content broadcast on this subject, so we are not going to go into detail here.

However, there are a few fundamentals we can introduce here that should underpin any project financing submission.

- Show the timeline and full amounts of your entire PFI (Project Finance Initiation) spend. Much of this can simply be travel and other expenses over and above actual acquisition of permits, architects drawings, legal fees and other costs. Keep a full and proper record of everything spent as this enhances the perception of your team's financial commitment to your project.

- Ensure that expenditure on construction etc match the costs shown in EPC, architects, project manager and other contracts and timelines. Any discrepancies will be immediately identified and challenged.

- Your revenue numbers need to reflect what shows in your off-take, licensing or similar agreements. Received wisdom is always to show worst case scenarios, but there are plenty of financiers who want to see best case as well. They will make their own judgement.

- When all your numbers are entered, show EBITDA from when your project starts operating and generating revenues up to the point where it has stabilised for three years.

- Remember that the funder will be seeking the same level of detail and professionalism on a $10 million project as they would on a $10 billion one. Do not cut corners.

Review, review and review

In the same way that the first three rules of marketing are *research, research* and *research*, the first three rules of project finance submissions are *review, review* and *review*.

Give it a week or two of refining, tweaking and enhancing before you submit. Have you made sure that the file names accurately reflect what they contain?; Are *all* your permits and permissions presented?; Are your feedstock, EPC, PPA/Offtake agreements fully prepared and, if not already, ready for signing?; Is your ES a compelling *summary* of your project for a busy *executive*?; Is the presentation of your ES and PP easy on the eye and written with clarity and focus?; Are the files organised in an intuitive and logical way in your Dropbox or in-house data-room?

If you can answer 'yes' to all of the above and those other questions that will be specific and unique to your project, then go ahead and click that 'send' button. But not before you have read and absorbed *Chapter 4: The Project Plan (PP)* and *Chapter 5: The Executive Summary and Submission*.

Should I tell the financier that we're shovel ready?

No. Keep it to yourself. Never announce that your project is 'shovel ready' in your submission.

Even better, find someone who does know what a project financing submission really entails, and ask them to assist you in bringing it up to the required 'submission ready' standard for you.

PFX NOTE

Some investors have a greater tolerance as to the state of 'submission/shovel readiness' than others.

When you raise your finance through PFX you give answers to a series of questions on your Intake Form which tells us at what stage of being submission ready you are. It also helps you get to that stage.

Naturally, you should be as close to 100% submission ready as possible, but sometimes there are contracts and agreements in progress that could delay your listing on PFX if you wait for them to be completed. PFX gives you the flexibility to move forward, but only if you are 100% sure that outstanding documentation will be available in an acceptable time-frame.

CHAPTER 4

THE PROJECT PLAN (PP)

+

This chapter should be read in conjunction with *Chapter 5: The Executive Summary (ES) and Submission*.

One of the most frustrating aspects of the job for financiers, their intake managers and analysts is the lack of a common standard for presenting applications for financing.

With the advent of Dropbox and other file sharing systems the whole process has changed significantly over the past two decades. Whereas once the PP would have been with annexes presenting all supporting documentation, these have now been replaced with Dropbox (or your own data-room) folders in which all those annexes are now placed. These can then be linked directly from the various headings in the PP.

It may seem a little strange putting the PP before the Executive Summary (ES) in this book. But it is essential to get this key document properly produced before editing it back to create the summary content the ES requires. And, from there, moving onto the submission.

The PP is the document that will make or break your application for project finance. If ever the funder is in doubt about something, this is where they will come for clarification.

While writing and assembling it, keep in mind that it will be read not only by the intake or deal origination executive but also, if you get past them, probably an investment committee, the underwriters, analysts, lawyers and others.

The following is a basic structure which has served the author well over four decades of venture, SME, corporate as well as, latterly, project financing.

How many pages your PP runs to is dictated solely by the type and complexity of your project.

But the first task is to convey on the cover page the 'what', 'where', 'who' and 'how much' of your project.

Project Plan

$780,000,000
Terms negotiable

India

Bridge and Transport Interchange

Submitted by

XXXXX Inc
Address: xxxxx
Main Contact:xxxxx
Phone: 000-000-0000 E-Mail: xxxxxxxx@xxxxxx.com

The sample cover page shown above is a wholly fictional example of how one should be produced. It conveys in an instant what the project is, where it is going to operate, what it is going to cost and who the project principals are. All presented on one page. With a cover like this, the funder will *want* to read what's behind it.

That old adage about a picture speaking a thousand words is true, and an image is absolutely essential. If it is a solar farm, then a generic image of which there are thousands available will suffice. The same applies to W2E plants, power stations, wind farms and similar projects.

However if it is a hotel, resort, hospital or similar 'custom' RE project then it is always best to use an image produced by the architect which shows the finished, built project in its best light.

Behind this cover page comes the contents page which, of course, is completed last. Before you set about compiling your PP be sure to set up page numbering on your document. Broadly speaking your contents page will cover the following:

- Introduction
- Permits and Permissions
- EPC Contractor and Summary of Terms
- Other Contractors and Project Participants
- Off-take/PPA/Licensing Entities and Structure (or Feasibility Study)
- Feedstock provider
- Land: Location, images, geo-surveys, ownership/options etc
- Financial Summary
- Annexes. See note on arranging Dropbox folders below.

Introduction

Write this so that there are no wasted words.

You have caught the attention of the funder with your cover page and, hopefully, a brilliantly produced ES (see *Chapter 5: The Executive Summary and Submission*) and you do not want to start boring them at the get-go. In this section you can explain the 'why' of your project.

On the project cover illustrated, the fictional story is that the bridge and interchange is being built to relieve existing congestion on the highway between two ports.

Take *your* project and write your own 'why'. Depending on the type of project you can add wider market statistics along with some key detail from your feasibility study. Or, if an energy project, some statistics (from an authoritative source) on the energy market in the country or region concerned.

But avoid the big mistake which so many project principals make, which is to cut and paste huge, yawn-inducing tomes from white papers, academic research and similar sources giving global market perspectives.

Indeed, this usually occurs when the submission is not for a project as such, but more for a speculative investment. Many times we receive what the client regards as a project, when it does not in fact meet project financing criteria. This can (sometimes) be overcome by securing pre-orders for your output from credible customers in order to qualify for project financing.

Give supporting background information that is relevant to *your* project alone.

Describe your project ensuring you embed all the following information in your text:

- What your project is
- Why you are embarking on it and what purpose/market it will serve (include highlights of feasibility study or other proof of demand for what you are building)
- When you started working on it (confirm how much you can prove you have spent on PFI costs)
- Who the company, team or SPV is driving it
- Where the project is located

You should also include information on any government, industry or other bodies that are supporting your project. Letters from such bodies should be added to the Annexes.

So, your Introduction should cover all the key elements of your project in as succinct a way as possible. Depending on the nature of the project this section can run from 500 to 1,000 words. Any more and the reader will start to lose interest, no matter how compelling your cover was.

Finally, you should use the Introduction to present any images or graphics that can further enhance your presentation. These include final renderings (other than used on the cover) and illustrations of your finished project.

Key Personnel
In this section provide 150 – 250 word summary bio's of those personnel that are going to be responsible for the three pillars of any enterprise (which will be c/p'd into your ES):

- Financial Control
- Sales, Marketing and Relationships
- Technical Knowledge

For the headline give the name, professional qualification(s) and job title, ie: 'John Smith CPA, CFO'. There might be more than three people when the CEO and COO are added, but you must show that you have these three key posts covered. It might also be that people from your EPC and Project Manager are supplementing your own in-house 'human assets', in which case they should also be included.

A mugshot for each one is sometimes helpful.

You should then include full cv's for these people in the relevant Dropbox folder.

Permits & Permissions
Every project is different but the following list should meet the needs of most. List all of them and show:

- Who issued them
- What dates they were issued

- The cost
- How long they are valid for

The following list, which is by no means definitive, covers different project sectors including energy and RE and will not apply to all projects nor to all countries. Also, it is important to understand that, even within countries, different states and provinces may well have their own permitting requirements.

Full copies should then all be included in the relevant Dropbox folder.

- Approval certificate
- Construction inspection schedule/notification
- Change of use permit
- Demolition permit Access and wayleaves for construction and operation
- Aeronautics permit (for projects being built near to airports)
- Approvals from utility providers
- Builders or construction company license
- Building Act compliance certificate
- Building and construction permit
- Certificate of Compliance (Design)
- Contractors
- Development permit
- Engineering and/or Architect License
- Environmental Impact Assessment

- Environmental Protection Certificate (for removal or use of hazardous materials)
- Environmental surveys and permits
- General Contractor License
- Grid access and connectivity
- Hazardous waste disposal approval
- Health, fire and safety surveys and permissions
- Land clearance licence
- Noise assessment
- Notice of Commencement of Works
- Permit for civil works
- Planning Permission or Consent
- Project start-up permission
- Reflection approval (solar farms)
- Socio-economic impact assessment/permit
- Town planning certificate
- Traffic effects study
- Tree felling permit
- Utility access and connection permissions
- Zoning permit (for architectural design)

EPC Contractor with Summary of Terms

Your EPC contractor, next to your off-taker and management team or company is top of the 'credibility' list for your funder. If yours is a major (say, $100million+) infrastructure, energy, RE or similar project they will need to be, as far as possible, a 'known' name.

For projects in the U.S., Canada, Australia and some other larger countries some EPC's who operate across just one or a few states or provinces will be quite adequate, depending on the nature of the project.

Are financiers just interested in facts and figures, or does it have to look nice as well?

Some of the largest project plans, for deals running into the $billions, have been so illiterate and unstructured that they have been impossible to read, hence binned.

Of course, it has to look nice.

Elsewhere, a leading national EPC can often be counted as acceptable if they can demonstrate the necessary track record and financial stability.

For the funder it is always useful to know if the EPC is listed on an exchange or carries a credit agency rating. If this is the case, make it clear in this section of your PP. Also, take relevant information from your EPC's site or corporate brochure and include it in your presentation. If they can show projects they have completed similar to yours include them in this section, which can be enhanced with an image or two of those completed projects, you should include them. The use of images is as much to maintain the reader's interest as to enhance the overall content of your PP.

Include a link to your EPC's website in this section and, if you feel it appropriate, their logo.

Also, you need to present the highlights of the agreement with your EPC. Point them to Annex 2 for the full agreement or MOU but bring out its key points in this section.

Show the project timelines and summary costs as provided by the EPC. Also, particularly (in the case of RE projects) the CPSF (cost per square foot), which is used as a yardstick to judge the value for money you are getting or the quality standards you want to build to.

Provide the Financier with all the information available on not just your EPC but others with specialist skills and experience.

If a performance bond is included, then show the details. If they are sub-contracting to others, show the complete list of sub-contractors. Some EPC's provide generic insurance policies which may or may not be useful or acceptable to the financier.

If they do, include these showing what they cover and who the underwriters are.

EPC contracts can carry a lot of '...subject to...' and '...in the event of...' clauses. Identify these and, where there are those that can be considered unique to your project (location, political environment, sector etc) bring these to the fore and clearly explain how these have been mitigated. Some can only be overcome when funding is actually approved and awaiting release and this might have to be worked through on your terms sheet.

It will save time if you highlight any issues you feel may delay your timeline to completion at the get-go. And also hold you in higher stead with the financier.

Other Contractors and Project Participants

For the funder to get a fully rounded picture of your project they need to know all key participants aside from your EPC contractor, which is deserving of having their own section in your PP.

Architects

For any project involving an element of RE which could be hospitals, hotels/resorts, airports, social housing and similar you are going to have an architect involved. It is therefore necessary to present them and their credentials in your PP. Show some completed projects, with images, and give the name of the individual(s) and professional qualifications of those you and your EPC will be dealing with in the firm. Include a link to their website.

Project manager

On some projects you will be using a project manager outside of your EPC. This usually happens where the project has a degree of specialism such as in airports, renewable energy, clinics and other sectors. They will work alongside your EPC and they can be contracted to or by the EPC. Present them here and include a link to their website.

Specialist equipment

Where you are using specialist equipment such as in renewable or O&G energy, hydro-electricity, wind turbines etc that are a key component of your project, present them here. While they may be sub-contracted to your EPC it is essential that their credentials are made known to the funder. Emphasis, as always, on track record and financial stability is crucial. Include a link to their website.

Off-take/PPA/Licensing Entities and Structure (or Feasibility Study)

Project finance means providing funding against the finished, built entity and the guaranteed/assured revenues it will deliver, thus enabling you to repay the debt provided. This is the component part of your project which decides for the financier whether or not you meet the requirements of 'project finance' as such, and if yours is a viable proposition for them.

In this section you need to present your off-taker, power purchaser, hotel, hospital or airport operator or whatever entity it is that has undertaken to guarantee that they are going to buy, lease or otherwise purchase what you are going to build or produce. Without it you do not have a project.

If you are reliant on a feasibility study, as with a hotel, airport, hospital and similar projects where revenues come from demonstrable market demand, then this is where you present the highlights.

Whether an off-taker or feasibility study you need to show credibility. For the off-taker, and as always, track record and financial stability are what the funder and their underwriters are looking for. In most cases this is not a problem as with energy the PPA is usually with a national or regional grid. Most hotel operators come with the necessary track record, hospital management companies and other off-takers as well usually present no issues for underwriters.

In the case of feasibility studies, the options are somewhat more limited. Whoever produces it, needs to show independence and, through many years of building their reputations, reliability in their projections and forecasts.

In the case of RE to tick that box for underwriters you need CBRE, Knight Frank or someone of similar pedigree. On transport and other infrastructure or, indeed any sector simply Google 'feasibility studies [sector]' and you will find what you are looking for.

However, before approaching any of them be sure to check out their backgrounds, track record and previous projects. Global operators will always carry more weight.

Include a link to your off-taker or feasibility study provider website.

Feedstock provider

The term 'feedstock provider' in itself is many faceted and can mean many things. It is most commonly used in W2E projects where municipal waste is fed into pyrolysis or similar processes with energy and by-products coming out the other end. This is a very simplistic description written with apologies to the army of pioneering engineers who are making all this possible.

A simpler process is where waste is incinerated but with the heat generated used to produce steam, which turns turbines, which powers generators, which produces electricity. This is not so efficient as pyrolysis and similar processes, as energy is consumed in the incineration at the start of the process.

In either case, the funder needs to know that there is surety of supply of feedstock to keep the plant operating. And this can be difficult, particularly in those countries where the collection and processing of waste is not particularly well structured and regulated.

The feedstock providers most acceptable to underwriters are those who are established names in waste processing for municipalities and local authorities such as Veolia, Suez, Clean Harbors, Waste Connections Inc, depending on where you are.

Some larger W2E companies such as Covanta also arrange their own feedstock through negotiating with waste generators and local authorities.

The key here is that, while there are countless companies with the capacity to recycle energy through waste, from the underwriting standpoint there is still a great deal of fragmentation in the collection and delivery of that waste (feedstock) to the plant itself. Be sure you have this fully covered and locked up tight before moving forward with your project financing.

Another feedstock sector is in the oil industry where it means the supply of crude to a refinery and then, at the end of the process, the supply of refined products to the oil storage depots, or tank farms, ready for distribution into the supply and retail networks. O&G is still a massive sector, and will remain so for at least the coming thirty years.

Renewable and stored energy is a long way from powering airliners, ships, heavy lifting gear, trucks, trains, mining equipment and all the other challenges it is not yet ready to meet.

Again, surety of supply is essential and contracts between oil producers and refineries, and then refineries, tank farms and their off-takers have to be prepared so that they can show this is the case.

As with all your other project participants, include a link to their website.

Land: Location, images, geo-surveys, ownership, options etc
Land can be the source of many problems and some of these are listed below:

- Land owner will not guarantee a 'holding' price with the project principals
- Project principals do not have the funds to buy an option on the land to fix a price
- Land owner (or their agents) will not produce a sale/transfer document without proof of funds to purchase
- Access difficulties via third parties
- Sale agreement has an expiry date that cannot be met by the financing process
- Vendor wants a deposit prior to completion of funding process

Any one of these issues can bring your financing to a juddering halt but, if you do not already own it, you have to show that you have control of it one way or another.

If you do not own it, one sure-fire arrangement the underwriter will accept is if you have a sale agreement that is 'subject to finance' and valid to a date nine months after signed agreement of final terms. Or, even better, buy an option that keeps the land 'yours' until you have closed your financing.

So the message is, along with all the other many issues presented in this chapter and elsewhere in this book, do not submit your application for project finance unless there are no loose ends on your land acquisition agreement with the vendor.

Or, put another way, until it is genuinely 'submission ready'.

Besides this you are going to need to show all the geo-surveys (where necessary), permits and permissions as previously mentioned in this chapter in Annex 6.

Financial Summary
For your PP, all that is needed is a high level summary including EBITDA for a time appropriate to your project. Simply extract the high level line items, leaving out the detail but sufficient for the funder to see quickly what is going out and what is coming in. They will look at the detail when they get to the full project spreadsheet you will include in the relevant Dropbox folder.

Who will proof read my project plan for me?

'Wordsmithing' is not a skill widely associated with engineering, financial control, design and construction. But ensuring that your PP is free of spelling and grammatical errors, and is not a challenge for the reader, is vital if it is to be taken seriously by potential financiers.

If you do not have someone on your team with these skills then pass it to someone who does, your PR person perhaps.

In this section you need to highlight two crucial pieces of information:

1. The Loan to Value (LTV) ratio. If you are looking to raise $90m of $100m all financial cost the LTV will be 90%. debt, depending on the project's circumstances.*
2. The Loan to Developed Value (LDV) ratio. If the finished, built project will be valued at $200m the LDV will be 45% (on $90m borrowed)

*Some financiers will offer 100% debt with an equity 'kicker'.

ANNEXES = DROPBOX/DATA-ROOM LINKS

Over time annexes have become replaced by Dropbox or in-house data-rooms with links to relevant folders direct from the various headings in your PP. Suggestions for organising your Dropbox are given at the end of *Chapter 5: the Executive Summary (ES) & Submission*. However, to provide a 'link' between how it used to be and how it now is, the following are some of the Annex/Dropbox titles/folder names.

Permits and Permissions

In this section you should include full and complete copies of all these documents and, as with all your documents, ensure that the file name reflects its contents unambiguously. If the document is the Environmental Impact Assessment issued by Anytown, make the file name: Anytown Environmental Impact Assessment (date). Remember, funders and their underwriters are very busy people and the easier you can make their lives the more they will warm to you.

File names issued by a scanning device show laziness on the part of the applicant and raise doubts in the reader's mind about your commitment to the project.

EPC and Other Contractor Agreements

This should include your entire complement of the EPC and all your other contractor agreements. It simply makes them easier to find. If available, it should also include company brochures for each contractor and links to their websites. Again, stick to the rule of unambiguous file names.   If the file is the EPC contract from Amalgamated Global Engineering, call it 'Amalgamated Global Engineering (AGE) EPC Contract'.   If it is their brochure, simply 'AGE Brochure'. Keep it simple.

PPA/Off-take/Licensing Agreements

These agreements can be lengthy, particularly PPA's and OMA's.   Wherever possible, also include corporate brochures or links to websites. All this will be asked for in any event by the underwriters, so best to give it to them all upfront.

And/Or...

Feasibility study where required (hotels, airports and similar)

Whoever provides your feasibility study should have long experience not only in the relevant sector but of producing the final document. This will have the key highlights/points demonstrating the viability of your project at the very start (sometimes the end), and this is what you should cut and paste under the same heading in your PP. Provided, of course, what they say is what you anticipated and what you really wanted them to say!

Key Personnel

While you've presented the summary bio's of your key personnel within the PP, this is where you should put their full *cv*'s.   Include employment and/or business career history, education and professional qualifications.

Land/Site

Besides whatever agreement you have with the current landowner, or the ownership documents, deeds or title to the land if you have them, you should include a Google Earth picture with the area you are going to develop or use marked off with a border. Where appropriate, this is the section where any agreements you have with utility providers should also be included with connection points highlighted on the image.

You can also use this image to show where you are connecting to the grid/power distribution network if appropriate.

Annex 6: Financials (Project .xls)

This is the honeypot for your financier and their underwriters. If you have got everything else in your PP right, this is where they will head straight to in order to ensure everything adds up. What they are looking for is absolute assurance that, based on the information you have provided throughout your PP your project, when it is finally built and operating, will deliver the revenues needed to repay the funding they will be providing you with.

Provide the file as an .xls, not .pdf, because they will be working with you on it to make sure it meets all their, and not just your, requirements.

By the time financing is finalised, it will look completely different.

This should be the crowning component part of your PP. If you have any doubts, keep at it until you are 100% sure that no holes can be picked in it.

PFX NOTE

Once you have engaged with a PFX Regional Manager they will provide all the assistance you need (within reason) in preparing your PP. The PP is sent to your Financier along with your contact and other company information when your PFX RM engages with the investor.

This is done only after they have spoken with those investors who have enquired about your opportunity and decided, with you, which is the most appropriate for you to move forward with.

The investor is advised that they will be contacted after three working days by PFX to set up your first call, from which point you can move forward.

CHAPTER 5:

THE EXECUTIVE SUMMARY (ES) AND SUBMISSION

+

I t is important to understand that probably the most frustrating part of the financier's (and their intake/ origination executives and analysts) jobs is the almost complete lack of understanding of how they work by those who approach them for funding.

This is probably because no-one has ever taken the trouble to tell them (until now). But, simply put, none of

them have the time nor, indeed, the inclination to spend hours working through entire, voluminous project plans to make an assessment for their particular funding structure.

They could be handling dozens of submissions every day and there simply is not the time to work through all those PP's or even ES's, all in different formats and styles, trying to find the key information they need. They want to grasp the thrust of your business or project swiftly and comprehensively.

So it is essential to master the art of writing an Executive Summary (ES) – that WORKS!

What is the point of the Executive Summary?

 You are producing a document for a busy **EXECUTIVE** to read in **SUMMARY** form conveying the key points of your project in a way that makes them want to learn more, and move onto your full PP.

You need to make an impression from the get-go.

There is a common trend among applicants to put the ES at the start of their PP. Sometimes it works, but most often it does not. We want to see the ES presented as a separate stand-alone document that we can quickly identify and read. In an ideal world, it will come attached to the initial e-mail enquiry.

Some ES's read more like novels or, even worse, sales brochures and many do not contain much of the information that a busy intake or origination executive needs to make that key 'yes' or 'no' decision.

Through your author's 30+ year career in project finance, there have been ES's that do not even show how much the client is seeking to raise.

Others, particularly in renewable energy, go into great detail about their solar or wind farm, or their waste to energy plant, and do not even say where it is going to be. Others present everything in Kw, Mw or even Gw output, as if they are in themselves a currency, with no actual mention of the actual money involved to make it all happen. None of this is made up!

The ES is the first the financier will see of you. It will either open the door for you, or have it slammed in your face. It's the easiest thing in the world to find an excuse to say 'no'. Don't provide that excuse through a poorly written ES.

In its most simplistic form, producing an ES as a lethal weapon in your project finance raising armoury amounts to utilising a long established public relations principle. In order to capture the attention of editors, every press release needs to embed (*not* list) the 'five-W's' into its opening paragraph.

These are: **Who, What, Where, Why and When.** But, as applied to your ES, the vital **HOW MUCH**, is added in at the start. Your ES should not run to any more than half a dozen pages. Ten at most:

For the front cover use the same as you used on your PP, but change 'Project Plan' to read 'Executive Summary'. There, you've got the 'who', 'what', 'where' and 'how much' across on one page, in one hit. The 'why' and 'when' can be presented within the ES.

Do not write the ES using the '5W's' as headings shown below, simply make sure that the information is embedded within your content.

1 WHAT: Describe what it is you are planning to do. Be it building a hotel, bridge, solar or wind farm or any other undertaking describe it in as few words as possible. The shorter the description the better it will always work.

Remember, the best propositions are always the simplest and easiest to explain. There is nothing wrong with including an illustration or other image of your project in this section, but only if it relates specifically to your project. Nothing generic.

2 HOW MUCH: This should come immediately after 'What' above. Even though you have already said it right up front on your cover it is absolutely critical to say how much funding is required within the body of your ES. This, after all, is what any funder wants to know from the get-go and, be absolutely assured, no gatekeeper or funder is going to read an entire PP (or even a poorly produced ES) in order to unearth this key piece of information.

It is advisable not to present how you want the financing structured. Always leave the structure 'open to negotiation'. By presenting your own, preconceived funding structure you will immediately close down dialogue with prospective financiers whose structure does not match what you are looking for, and who might well be able to offer you an alternative, better deal.

> *"You are producing a document for a*
> *busy EXECUTIVE to read*
> *in SUMMARY form"*

Immediately below your 'how much' you need to present those three crucial pieces of information which a financier looks out for right up front:

1. Forecast post-stabilization EBITDA, ie::

	Year 1	Year 2	Year 3	Year 4	Year 5
Turnover					
EBITDA					
	%	%	%	%	%

2. The Loan to Value (LTV) ratio. If you are looking to raise $90m of $100m all financial cost the LTV will be 90%.

3. The Loan to Developed Value (LDV) ratio. If the finished, built project will be valued at $200m the LDV will be 45%.

Thus, *in just one minute*, with your front cover and first paragraph inside the ES you have shown the investor what you are doing (in a little more detail than on your cover page), how much it is going to cost and whether your EBITDA is able to support the funding terms they can offer.

Producing Your Executive Summary

When you are settled and happy with your wordage, take the time to make sure it looks good and spend time on the production.

There is no point working hard on producing a compelling, exciting ES if the presentation is a dog's dinner. Remember, yours is not the only ES the reader is looking at.

This advice applies equally to your PP.

You've achieved your primary objective: **Grabbed their attention by answering their key questions right up front**. Then...

3 WHERE: Is your enterprise going to service a particular country, region within a country or is it being prepared for world domination? Again, explain in as few words as possible, all the detail will be in your full PP which the funder will want to move onto after reading your ES (if you've done it right!).

4 WHO: Lift your summary management bio's from your PP and drop them into your ES. Again, be sure you have those three pillars of any successful enterprise covered, ie: 1) technical/product knowledge; 2) sales/marketing and 3) financial control. If any one of those pillars is missing, it is a given that your project will fail.

5 WHEN: Have you already bought the site and cleared it, do you need to meet a specific start date and, if so, what reason or is your project dependent on funding before you can make a start on it? If you are restricted to a start date then it is absolutely essential that you give the funder plenty of notice, as in many months. They will not be pressured into trying to meet unrealistic timelines. A project financing can take anywhere from three to nine months, depending on the structure and, sometimes, even more.

Make your time frames clear but *never, ever* say you are up against a deadline which will give your submission the kiss of death.

6 WHY: Why is your project viable? Why do you believe that what you want funded is actually going to produce enough profit to provide an equity investor with attractive enough returns or a lender to be assured the loan is going to be repaid?

Present here the most relevant points of your feasibility study, the highlights from your PPA, OMA or other agreement that will 'underwrite' the viability of your project. Simply state who the agreements are with (include links to their website) and how long they are for. No need to go into intricate detail at the ES stage. If you are reliant on a feasibility study, a *very* short 'highlights' synopsis of its content is what is needed here.

Avoid committing the most common mistake of all, which is going into long and lengthy detail about the size of your global market, projections for its growth and comments from learned bodies and individuals about its potential. Nothing is more guaranteed to produce a yawn from the reader. If you have to include anything of this nature, keep it to a few sentences with links to your sources.

THE SUBMISSION
After all the time effort and money you have spent on preparing your application, it would be tragic to mess everything up by getting this last, critical stage of your project finance raising process wrong.

So often we receive e-mails with a rambling message pointing us to a collection of attachments, often with meaningless file names and, amongst which, we cannot even find an ES. Even worse, simply a link to the project's website.

We might see 'Project Plan' or 'Business Plan' but when we open it we are looking at a disorganised chaos of unstructured information, with the sender wondering why they get a 'not interested' message within a day or two.

It is important that you 'go retrospective' and see everything in this entire process from the financier's point of view.

Never mind what you want to tell them, ensure that it is told in a way that is easy and convenient to absorb and understand. And the submission process follows those key principles.

We need to get a move on, can I make the funder move faster?

You will fail at the first hurdle if to tell the funder that your application is urgent or time-critical.

Yours is not the only project in the world and you are effectively telling the funder you do not know how to plan.

Step 1: Organise Your Files
The financier could be handling dozens of transactions at any one time, see this from their point of view. Pick a six-digit code for your transaction (as near as possible to an

acronym of your project title, and prefix every file with that code. So, if your project is a hospital in Brazil pick, say, 'HOSBRA'.

All this means is that when your file is being passed around between analysts, underwriters, lawyers and others within your funding group, it is much easier for them to identify out of all their other current transactions. It's easy enough to do. Right click the file name and you will see 're-name' as one of the options. If you've dozens of files it could get a bit tedious, but it will be well worth it at the end of the day.

Step 2: Load up Dropbox (or your own data-room)

 You need to get your entire collection of files loaded onto Dropbox, or your own data-room ready for your financier to come calling. Organise your files in a logical and intuitive way. All projects are different and the following example is by no means set in stone. Using the hospital in Brazil example above, organise your Dropbox files as follows:

▓ **FOLDER: INTAKE DOCUMENTS**
   ▓ HOSBRA Brazil hospital ES
   ▓ HOSBRA Brazil hospital Project Plan
   ▓ HOSBRA Sponsor/SPV/Company registration, tax and other compliance documents
   ▓ HOSBRA Past three years balance sheets (if available)

FOLDER: Annex 1: Permits and Permissions

- HOSBRA [Municipality/authority] environmental impact certificate
- HOSBRA [Municipality access permission]
- HOSBRA [Municipality land clearance permission]
- HOSBRA [Municipality land use and construction permit]

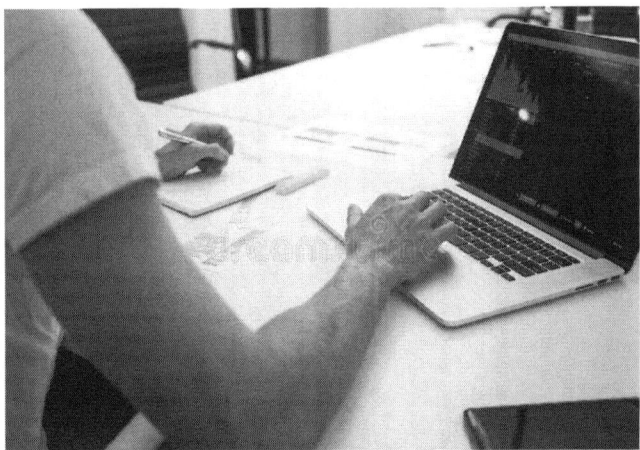

What used to be annexes on the Project Plan are now links to your Dropbox or in-house data-room folders.

FOLDER: Annex 2: EPC and other contractor agreements

- HOSBRA EPC (ie: Amalgamated Engineering Group (AEG)) Contract
- HOSBRA EPC AEG corporate brochure
- HOSBRA Note: if your EPC contractor has key/major subcontractors you may want to include these in this folder.

FOLDER: Annex 3: PPA/Off-take

- HOSBRA PPA or other off-take agreement
- HOSBRA Other off-take or further revenue generating agreements.

OR

FOLDER: Annex 3: Operations & Management Agreement (OMA)

- HOSBRA Hotel, airport, hospital etc OMA
- HOSBRA Further revenue generating agreements

FOLDER: Annex 4: Key Personnel

- HOSBRA CV files for each project leader

FOLDER: Annex 5: Feasibility study where required (hotels, airports and similar)

- HOSBRA [Name of study producer] Feasibility Study

FOLDER: Annex 6: Land/Site

- HOSBRA Google Earth image of site
- HOSBRA Land ownership document (or sale contract/option etc)

FOLDER: Annex 7: Financials (Project master .xls plus those from providers in Annex 2 if appropriate)

- HOSBRA Full project financials

The foregoing is a non-definitive guide to how you should organise and present your files on Dropbox, use it as a template (choosing your own six-digit project code) for your own project.

Step 3: The E-Mail

This is the moment your entire team has been working towards. After checking, re-checking (and re-checking again) all your files in all your Dropbox or dataroom folders you are now ready to present yourself to the funder.

Again, see it from their viewpoint. Short, sharp, to the point and as much information in as short a time as possible.

It is always worth a phone call to identify someone within the financier, if you have not already, to who the e-mail should be sent. If you're working with a seasoned intermediary, they will be able to handle all this for you.

This is what all your hard work comes down to at the end of the day:

SUBJECT: Hospital. Brazil. $170 million. (HOSBRA)

Dear [name if you have one – always best to call first and get one after you've thoroughly researched what the invsestor's preferences]:

Please find attached the Executive Summary for our proposed hospital construction project in Sao Paulo, Brazil. We believe we have secured all necessary permits, permissions, EPC, off-take and other contracts and agreements to make the project a viable proposition for [name of financier].

If you find the attached of interest please contact me directly so that we can prepare an NDA. After which I will send you the link to our Dropbox where all project files are organised for your easy access and review.

We look forward to hearing from you in due course.

Kind regards

Etc.

Asking for Proof of Funds

 Many government departments along with other project principals around the world insist on seeing proof of funds before engaging with a financier they do not know. For most private debt and equity providers this is impossible as their funds are aggregated from many different *private* sources, not one central 'pot'.

PFX NOTE

 PFX creates your ES for you using information provided by you in your oirignal documentation, and enhanced in our subsequent interaction with yu. This is then sent in response to Online Registered investors who click the 'Request Executive Summary' button on your Elevator Pitch.

They can then download the full executive summary direct from the site.

Alternatively, a growing number of larger investors are registering under the PFX Concierge program, where we monitor and navigate PFX for them. When suitable deals are listed, these Concierge investors are notified directly and personally and given first refusal on deals.

CHAPTER 6:
FINANCING STRUCTURES

+

I t would be impossible to find every conceivable structure within the pages of the hundreds of books, courses and seminars that have been produced on the subject.

Which is why we are not going to try and review them all here.

Due to the sheer volume of financiers it would be impossible to review every single structure available. However, the start point was In *Chapter 1: Introduction* where we separated institutional from private finance providers.

The overwhelming majority of U/HNWI's deploy their cash across public equities, pension, mutual, fixed income and other institutions, where their funds are largely protected by the 'A' rated investments those institutions are limited to. Which restricts the returns, as well as the investment opportunities, for the institutions themselves.

Having protected that proportion of their wealth they do not want to risk losing, U/HNWI's will then deploy whatever is left across their wealth manager, alternative investment manager, family office, asset manager, hedge fund or whatever other private (risk-inclined) investment channels they choose.

Historically, these investments have been predominantly equity but, as banks have retreated from the market, private debt has taken a lead position.

The consensus among market participants and commentators is that private capital, be it debt or equity, is set to dominate the market for decades to come.

Indeed the sheer weight of private capital is going to transform the entire global banking firmament. No-one has quite yet worked out how.

This is the primary source of capital for the overwhelming majority of projects. Unfortunately there is no central database of them and each operates in a fragmented, unstructured and hopelessly inefficient market, mostly with their own individual financing structures and subjective preferences for deal size, sector and location.

If we add them all up across single and multi-family offices, wealth managers, private banks (now many also acting as wealth managers), private capital, direct investment, private debt/equity, asset manager and hedge funds along with other entities that essentially provide the same service, we can only guess at between 50,000 and 100,000 of them serving some twenty million U/HNWI's worldwide.

Will there be any personal liability?

 Genuine project finance is non-recourse, meaning that the financing is secured against the contracted revenues the finished, built project is going to generate, usually through a special purpose vehicle (SPV).

Hence there is no personal liability on the project principals.

It is impossible to assess how many of these U/HNWI's are actually active project finance debt or equity investors through whichever channel they are using. But a conservative estimate would be between one quarter and one third. Say, five to 6.5 million of them deploying an estimated aggregate of $5 to $6.5 trillion. A huge, shifting market with countless permutations of structures and mandates.

So, in this chapter we are not going to review all the variations there are on private debt and equity project financing. If anybody ever did attempt it they would probably never get it finished and nobody would read it anyway.

The best way to explain what to expect in a terms sheet from a private debt or equity provider is set out below as an amalgamation of a number structures taken from the author's files.

It covers energy as well as other sectors and it assumes the reader is able to identify what would be most applicable to them.

Apologies (again) in advance to the purists and technical experts who will have conflicting views on the following presentation.

It is intended as a high level, introductory guide for those preparing to bring their projects to market.

PRIVATE DEBT AND EQUITY PROJECT FINANCE STRUCTURES OVERVIEW

Equity
- Agreed at the outset or converted from an element of the debt, perhaps a mezzanine portion of the total debt.
- Possibly conditional on a default clause.

Tranches
- Funds are released over the construction period in agreed amounts.
- Usually spread over the construction period with tranches drawn down through certificates issued by architects or EPC contractor.

- Depending on the financiers structure funds are released either through an escrow account, direct from the funder or through the SPV bank account on the financier's instructions.

Interest and Term (Tenor)

- Term is usually calculated with the interest against the PPA, off-take, OMA or similar agreement to ensure repayments are manageable.
- Interest may be different rates for different component parts of the funding
- Tenor will depend on the nature of the project and can run between five and 20 (or more) years.
- Early-settlement thresholds, with an exit or redemption fee, can usually be built into the agreement. However, keep in mind that specialist project financiers like long term debt as this delivers the preferred long-term return for them, so early redemption is not always the preferred option for the funder.

Repayment Options

- There is often a grace period for capital and interest during the construction period, although sometimes they are rolled up and added to the loan from the point where repayments are scheduled to start

- Principal can be repaid with interest over the repayment period
- A separate sinking fund can be established (or an instrument issued) which repays capital at the end of the period
- Capital and/or interest payments can be paid monthly, quarterly, semi-annually or annually (rarely) in arrears
- Can be geared to meet growing revenues as project output gears up

Security

This usually comes in the form of charges and debentures over the assets of the project and, sometimes the assets of not just the SPV but also the applicant company and those providing design and contracting input (usually covered by their corporate and professional indemnity insurance policies).

This is dependent on the risk profile of the project. However, genuine project financing should not include personal guarantees.

Conditions Precedent (CPs)

This is the list of requirements, by no means definitive, to be met prior to financial close:

- Sight and approval of EPC and all other contracts
- Approval of OMA, PPA or other 'off-take' agreement(s) by funders own professional advisors

- Sight and approval of all permits, permissions, wayleaves and other documentation confirming that the project has met all statutory requirements from the local, regional or national issuing authority
- Copies of Board resolutions as appropriate
- Confirmation that guarantees and performance bonds are in place
- Confirmation that the SPV executive has rights of execution
- Approved report on environmental, technical, access and other matters by professional advisors
- Confirmation from auditors that the financial model is approved
- Valuation appraisal/feasibility report of the property by surveyor/valuer approved by the funder
- Confirmation of LTV ratio
- Proof of title/ownership certificates of all project properties
- Financier's review of all technical, environmental, insurance, taxation and legal due diligence, voting rights, where applicable are in place

Information Requirements

Once the funds have been released, and then when the project is operating, you may be required to provide the funder with key items of information:

- Financial and logistical reports on the construction stage of the project
- Semi-annual or annual reports on the operating project
- Monthly, quarterly or as appropriate reports on the construction and logistical progress of the project
- Copies of all fulfilment certificates, including completion tests issued by suppliers and the financier's technical advisor(s).
- Annual financial reports on the operating performance of the project for the coming year.
- Notice of any material loss or damage
- Notice of any disputes under any of the project agreements
- Claims, potential or actual litigation, breach, variation or termination of, or right to terminate or dispute under any of the project agreements
- Details of claims, litigation, arbitration or other similar proceedings commenced or threatened by a third party against the project principals, the SPV or any project party by a third party
- Indemnity claims made pursuant to any of the project agreements.

Language

Particularly in Latin America where Spanish and Portuguese are prevalent we find whole submissions coming from that region in those languages.

While it is a legal requirement that documentation is produced in the native language of the jurisdiction, project financing is a global market.

Documents need to be translated into English and notarised.

Default events

Standard terms typical to project finance transactions include the following:

- Failure to make payments
- Breach of agreements and covenants
- Statements, undertakings and warranties found to be misleading or untrue
- Change of control or other material circumstances for the borrower
- Default in respect of other financial commitments
- Client abandons project

- Insolvency, bankruptcy or similar circumstances of project principals and/or counterparties
- Nationalisation or other adverse political circumstance
- Sale of project assets without notice to agreement by lender
- Security or guarantee found to be invalid

Fees and margins

These will all be clearly set out in the term sheet and will include:

- Upfront (arranging and underwriting) fees
- Legal, technical and other professional (third party) fees (including due diligence)
- Allow a total of between $100,000 and $500,000 (sometimes less, sometimes more)
- All fees are usually paid to the financier, not because they want to make a margin when they pay onto their professional advisors (third parties), but so that they *know* the fees have been paid and can start to work directly with them to take your project forward.

Depending on the lender and their structure, there may well be other elements to the term sheet covering hedging (usually to cover FX issues), Debt Service Reserve Account, Maintenance Reserve Accounts, Sinking Fund.

CHAPTER 7

FINANCIER TYPES AND HOW TO FIND THEM

+

As we discussed in *Chapter 1: History and Introduction*, the market has evolved to a point where we have a whole range of financier types all performing, essentially, the same function of directing private capital into projects that need financing.

Within that range there are those that have evolved out of entities that originated back in the 1970's and 1980's and others that have emerged in more recent times. We will make all this clear as we work through them below, in alphabetical order.

We will also provide some guidance on how to track down and approach them with your project, once you have prepared it as presented in Chapters 3, 4 and 5 of this book. Before you start, be prepared for a long and time consuming process, which you should start on at the very earliest stages of your project's gestation:

Alternative Investment Managers/Funds

The Alternative Investment Management Association, AIMA, represents the global alternative investment industry. Its membership is focused very much on hedge funds but, in reality 'alternative investment' is now represented by a whole plethora of different entities.

In my previous book published in 2011, *ALTERNATIVE CAPITAL RAISING – Business Funding in the New Capital Markets,* (co-authored with Arianne Richter and long since overtaken by events) we highlighted '*The Impact of Private Wealth*' in Chapter 2. And, at least in that sense, nothing has changed and it is worthwhile extracting and re-iterating some of that content here:

> **"Alternative capital era**
>
> We can see new financing structures becoming established on an almost weekly basis, without exception working to entirely different rules and principles with which we were once all familiar.
>
> The people are different too. There used to be offices filled with administrators processing business loan applications, or working to pre-set debt/equity structures based on long established

principles. In more recent years venture capital and private equity firms started to jostle with hedge funds to identify what are now known to them as 'alternative investments' but which are, in reality, *your*...project finance opportunities. These are funded through the diverse range of funding instruments and channels that now define the alternative capital market.

The traditional established private equity, venture capital and business loan market is rapidly declining. Although in some regions of the world it would be more accurate to say it is still there, but without the financial resource it used to have to actually do any serious business. Their position can be likened to one of those cartoon characters running off the edge of a cliff and hanging in mid-air for a few moments, before plummeting into the gorge below. (**Author:** *this has since demonstrably been the case*).

We are now in the alternative capital era and it is led by a stratum of financial innovators. They have brought trading, structuring and other experience gained at the highest levels of the global capital markets to bear on mainstream business finance and project funding deals.

It is these new funding structures and programs being generated by the alternative capital market that are already funding more projects, to greater deal values, than traditional sources. For investors in these funds be they private, corporate or institutional this new global structure delivers greater risk spread, retained liquidity and far more flexibility than the old, traditional private equity structures.

These deals are not publicised as the strict client confidentiality that has always prevailed, rightly, across the 'high finance' market, now applies to mainstream corporate and project finance in the alternative capital market. (**Author**: *also many of the structures are proprietary thereby demanding confidentiality*).

...

Business angels

The first real manifestation of alternative capital in its most primitive form was the business angel movement that began in 1995.

Business angels are essentially entrepreneurs doing what they instinctively do by way of investing in what they perceive to be a wealth creating opportunity.

They do it when the opportunity arises, if that opportunity fits their current outlook and, key to the decision, if it is money they can afford to lose.

That said, the business angel movement demonstrated that it was not the capital itself that was alternative, money is money no matter how you look at it. But rather than the entrepreneur leaving his money in a fund to be invested on his behalf, he would have it working for him as a direct investment in what he regards as a good judgement call driven by the risk *v* reward dynamic.

So, the money was not invested through a managed fund (which would never go near the kind of risk profile an entrepreneur would anyway), but directly by the entrepreneur himself after conducting his own due diligence and negotiating his own terms.

Therefore, it is the *route* (*Author: to this might now be added 'and structure'*) **the capital takes to the investment that is alternative, and not the capital itself. That, along with greater 'risk inclination' is what defines the new, global Alternative Capital Market."**

Although written in 2011, this analysis of the market still stands and, when applied particularly to the project finance market, is even more relevant. In today's market what we present here as Alternative Investment Managers/Funds can broadly be described as hedge funds, asset managers or, perhaps, private equity/debt funds. There is a LOT of overlap. In all cases, they are managing private capital on behalf of wealth managers, family offices, U/HNWI's, sovereign wealth funds or the many other sources of private wealth.

Do a search on 'alternative investment managers' and, as with any prospective financier you find, regardless of what 'type' they go under, be sure that what you have to offer is what they are actually looking for by way of market sector, location and deal value.

Asset Managers

Wikipedia defines asset management as: *"...the systematic approach to the governance and realization of value from the things that a group or entity is responsible for, over their whole life cycles. It may apply both to tangible assets and to intangible assets."*

Originally, the focus was on physical assets for governments, utilities, municipalities, major corporations and, sometimes, smaller or mid-size corporate entities. In more recent times, however, there has been a notable incursion into the project finance market by 'asset managers' who have taken a far more focused approach to, perhaps, the 'intangible assets'.

ValueWalk's 'Rankings of the Largest Asset Management Companies' (published in 2020) shows the following listing.

10- Amundi
Asset Management, $1.59 trillion

French asset management giant Amundi had EUR 1.425 trillion ($1.59 trillion) of assets under management at the end of 2018, making it one of the world's largest asset management companies. It was formed in 2010 following the merger of the asset management businesses of Societe Generale and Credit Agricole. It has offices in 37 countries. It operates mutual funds, ETFs, real estate and private equity funds.

9- BNY Mellon, $1.7 trillion

The Bank of New York Mellon is one of the world's oldest banks with its roots going back to 1784, when Alexander Hamilton founded the Bank of New York. Its asset management arm has $1.7 trillion of assets under management, according to the company's regulatory filing. BNY Mellon was formed in 2007 following the merger of the Bank of New York with Mellon Financial.

8- Capital Group Companies, $1.86 trillion

Founded in 1931, Capital Group Companies had $1.86 trillion of total assets under management as of March 2019. It has more than three dozen mutual funds through its subsidiary American Funds. Capital Group Companies has a strong presence not only in the US but also in Asia, Europe, and South America. The company has also been praised for the diversity among its employees.

7- Allianz, $2.19 trillion

German insurance and asset management giant is the largest asset management company in Europe. According to the company's regulatory filing, it had $2.19 trillion of assets under management at the end of 2018. Allianz's asset management business consists of PIMCO, Allianz Global Investors, and Allianz Real Estate. Yes, PIMCO is a wholly-owned subsidiary of Allianz.

6- Fidelity Investments, $2.56 trillion

Led by billionaire Abigail Johnson, Fidelity Investments has $2.56 trillion in assets under management, making it one of the world's largest asset management companies. Fidelity ContraFund and Fidelity 500 Index Premium are two of its most popular mutual funds. Fidelity also offers brokerage services. Last year, it started offering mutual funds with zero expense ratio.

5- JPMorgan Chase, $2.73 trillion

New York-based JPMorgan Chase is one of the world's largest banks. It also offers a wide range of services such as asset management, investment banking, brokerage, credit cards, and treasury & security services. At the end of 2018, it had $2.73 trillion in assets under management.

JPMorgan Chase was formed in 2000 following the merger of JPMorgan with Chase Manhattan.

4- State Street Global Advisors, $2.81 trillion

Boston-based State Street Global Advisors is a subsidiary of State Street Corporation. It had $2.81 trillion in AUM at the end of 2018. It manages money for local governments, associations, educational institutions, non-profits, and even religious organizations. The SSGA was founded in 1978. It offers asset management services in countries across the Americas, Europe, and Asia.

3- Charles Schwab, $3.52 trillion

Charles Schwab is a leading banking and brokerage services provider in the United States. It also provides asset management, margin lending, and other services. Charles Schwab has more than 11 million active brokerage accounts and $3.52 trillion of assets under management. Charles Schwab is known for bringing investing to the masses through low commissions and an electronic trading platform.

2- Vanguard, $5.2 trillion

Founded by legendary investor John Bogle, The Vanguard Group is credited with popularizing low-cost passive investing. Its funds mirror the asset allocation of an index or the broader stock market without the involvement of an active fund manager. That's why its expense ratios are much lower than active funds. According to Vanguard, it had $5.2 trillion in total assets at the end of January 2019.

1- BlackRock, $6.5 trillion

New York-based BlackRock is by far the world's largest asset management company with AUM of $6.5 trillion as of April 2019, according to the company's regulatory filing. Founded in 1988, BlackRock is often referred to as the world's largest shadow bank due to its mammoth size and power. BlackRock's iShares funds are incredibly popular among individual investors as well as businesses. BlackRock funds focus on risk management, which is why they performed much better than others during the 2008 financial crisis.

Source: ValueWalk

Out of all these 'asset managers' there is not one where the review mentions anything to do with physical assets. Although their project financing activities may well create a great many physical assets. But it is still a stretch to define themselves as 'asset managers'.

With all these names the first word that comes to mind is 'bank', or 'finance'. This is not out of any attempt to misrepresent themselves, simply a result of the confusion that has come about through the tectonic changes to the market, and its make-up, over the past decade.

What are presented here as 'Asset Managers' could just as easily be described as Alternative Investment, Private Equity/Debt managers or, even, Hedge Funds.

Only the top ten are presented in the ValueWalk table above, all of which are only interested in deals of real substance. Infrastructure, energy and hotel/resort deals with, usually, an absolute minimum value of $100 million, but more likely upwards of $250 million. But a search on 'asset managers' followed by your location on Google could well produce smaller firms closer to you that could be interested in your project.

Or there are plenty of people selling lists of them.

Corporate Lenders/Investors
This is a much overlooked source of project finance. There are many medium-to large-size corporations operating across hotels, energy, shipping, infrastructure and other major project finance sectors that are always on the look-out for opportunities.

It may be that they do not have the full funding requirement, but could well have financing relationships that they could bring to bear.

The best way to find them is to have your PR person prepare a press release, naturally with an attractive image of the finished project, to send to the specific industry media. Keep it short, sharp and to the point, preferably no more than 300-500 words (which enhances its chances of being used as a news item). This is what used to be called (back in the day) 'Investor Relations'.

Be it road, rail, solar, bridges, waste-to-energy (or any other renewable), hotels and resorts and all other sectors, there will be a plethora of media serving that market. You will be able to find national, regional and global media serving every sector. Track them down, find the relevant editor or journalist and build your list (e-mail and phone).

Aside from sending the press release, you should also follow up with a call to the editor or journalist. Ask if they got the press release and, if not, offer to send it again. *Always* ensure you have an attractive and photogenic image to send in (preferably) high resolution and (most definitely) colour. Do that and you are halfway to getting your column inches.

In the first paragraph be sure to embed the 'what', 'where', 'who', 'why' and 'when' of your project and, especially, the 'how much' your project is going to cost (as previously described in *Chapter 5: The Executive Summary (ES) and Submission*. In the other paragraphs be sure to include a little about your management team, confirm that all permits and permissions are secured and any further information you feel may be key to pulling a response out of the media's audience.

Keep in mind also that financiers of whatever description also read industry media relevant to their particular sector interests.

Hedge Funds

Currently, probably the most prolific and diverse source of private capital available. As with most other investor types, they must work within the rules they set with their private capital sources – their investors. Probably more than any other investor type they target to deliver market-leading returns for their investors which does not in any way mean that they are prepared to take market-leading risks.

As with any other funding source they will conduct extensive due diligence and evaluate your project to the *nth* degree. If you have followed the guidelines presented in this book, you will stand a better chance than most of establishing a relationship with the right person in the fund and taking your project through to closing.

You can do your own search on Google, or buy your list from someone like EurekaHedge or Preqin which provide a global lists (from which you can select regions if you wish). There are also other, regional, offerings which all cost money but, if you are serious about your project, it could be money well spent.

The information which comes with most lists includes sectors of interest, preferred deal values and, sometimes, a little about the financing structures the fund uses.

Investment Banks

As mentioned in Chapter 1, Investment Banks, which made their presence felt most heavily in the 1970's merged with or morphed into private debt and equity, and then hedge funds by the end of the 1980's. Look for a list of Investment Banks now, and it will look very similar to a list of asset managers, private equity or hedge funds.

Which shows just how messy this market has become. And why it is best to lock into a seasoned intermediary or gatekeeper who knows their way around.

Mandated Lender

This is a recent arrival which your author believes will make a significant impact as time goes on, particular in the middle-value band.

These are individuals or small teams who have relationships with private banks, wealth managers, family offices, U/HNWI's, corporations and others. They can identify financing opportunities and, critically, make the investment decision without needing to refer back to their 'members'. They have the mandate to structure and execute the deal.

Your author came across a small raft of these with a search on 'private capital lenders' followed by the relevant region in the UK. This has since been tried on various regions in North America, Europe and Australasia with notable success.

Broadly speaking the lending criteria appeared to be a mix of private equity and debt and, most often, within the $20 to $500 million band, but sometimes more. Debt rates appear to be a tad over current market.

Pension/Fixed Income or other institutions

Unless you are a major corporation, municipality or another entity that can show a Moody's, S&P or Fitch rating these sources are not for you. The key difference between such institutions and private capital lenders/investors is that they are responsible for other people's money such as pensions, life policies, mutual and other fixed-income funds which have to be, as far as humanly possible, risk-free.

If you do work with such institutions, you have no need of this book.

Private Banks and/or Wealth Managers

On the great scale of things, a recent development that has gathered a little momentum over the past decade. Private Banks and Wealth Managers used to have their own turf but, as with Investment Banks and Hedge Funds they have, in many cases, morphed into one.

If you talk to hedge funds, mandated lenders or private equity/debt funds, these are usually the channels that private banks and/or wealth managers will invest in on behalf of their clients.

Private Equity and/or Debt Manager/Fund

Again, another tale of morphing and shifting definitions. Many readers will recall the supersonic rise of the PE fund back in the 1990's. Essentially, these funds would take a company, reinforce the balance sheet with equity, then leverage that up with additional debt to take the company forward.

The debt would come from banks, who could make a reasonable lending judgement based on the (now reinforced) balance sheet, together with the company's history and future prospects. Sometimes it worked, sometimes it did not because of over-leveraging. But, as time went on, the debt source started to come from private capital.

The huge flow of capital out of the mainstream banks and into what the financial establishment began to refer to as 'shadow banking' after the 2008 crash created a fundamental shift in how private equity worked.

Now, most of those that started out as Private Equity funds are now Private Equity and Debt funds, sourcing the funding from the whole gamut of private capital sources.

If you do a search on 'private equity and debt' you will find a great deal of duplication with Hedge Funds and Asset Managers. However, PE/Debt tends to lean more towards corporate lending rather than project finance and the recommendation would be to steer away from this lending type.

Single-/Multi-Family Office/U & HNWI

 While in Chapter 1, we say that this is the new kid on the block, it is actually the *ultimate* source of *all* private capital.

The so-called 'fat cats'. Ultra & High Net Worth Individuals (U/HNWI's) and their family offices are overwhelmingly self-made people with entrepreneurial instincts and a risk-inclined attitude to investment.

They will usually manage their wealth by depositing a good proportion in safe, institutional vehicles, spreading some across hedge funds and asset managers and keeping a proportion for their own discretionary investments.

HNWI's are generally defined as anyone with more than $1 million of liquid cash over and above their home(s), cars, boats or any other assets. There is no broadly accepted definition for *Ultra*-HNWI's although there are those who say this refers only to billionaires of which (at the time of writing) there about 2,500 in the world, many of which are multi-billionaires. However there is a huge stratum of HNWI's verging on billionaire status, perhaps as many as 20,000 with upwards of $100 million to approaching the necessary $1,000 billion.

Until the beginning of the 2010's, a family office was hardly heard of, let alone a multi-family office, so to sub-define the two:

Family office

The private office of a wealthy family, usually built from wealth grown over one or more generations from a family business. It will manage all the family's affairs including legal, financial and what might be described as concierge.

Multi-family office

These are set up to provide family office resources to a number of wealthy individuals or families across the same legal, financial and concierge elements. These are contracted primarily by those families that cannot justify an office of their own, but nevertheless need this support to manage their affairs properly.

Until very recently, these offices would direct their 'risk-inclined' capital through hedge funds, asset managers and others. However, there has been a recent trend towards the larger family offices doing it for themselves.

Many of the 'known' billionaires now have family offices that operate along the lines of asset managers, hedge, private equity and venture capital funds.

Again, until recently, their approach to investing for themselves was noticeable only by their lack of the real professional demands involved with project finance. But, now, those professionals are being recruited from the various financier types to build up the necessary expertise those family offices need.

Their investment preferences are not always towards project finance. Aside from the few dozen top tier family offices, investment in this sector is through the other channels mentioned in this chapter.

Also, the UHNWI's they represent have usually built their wealth from entrepreneurial activity in a specific sector, from which they do not usually deviate. However, in time, this situation could well change, at which point there will be yet more morphing and merging!

Family offices are not *yet* a viable source of project financing, mostly because they are so difficult to identify and prefer to work through people already known to them. But it would be fair to speculate that they will overtake some other investor types as defined in this chapter over the coming decade.

SUMMARY

In summary, to identify prospective financiers for your project follow the guidance above and focus your efforts on Asset Managers, Corporate Lenders, Hedge Funds, and Mandated Lenders.

But, be sure to follow the submission readiness, executive summary, project plan and other advice given elsewhere in this book if you want to be taken seriously by any of them.

The following is a short list of potential sources of private capital financing, but it is important to emphasise that should you wish to contact any of them, it is best to phone first and get a contact to talk to and start building a relationship with:

Preqin. www.preqin.com
Lists available across all investor types including family offices, hedge funds, private equity funds etc

Hedge Fund Databases. www.eurekahedge.com
A list of almost 26,000 hedge funds, asset managers and private debt/equity providers

Family Office List. https://familyofficelist.org
Founded in 2001 by a specialist in the U/HNWI financial services.

List of Asset Managers.
www.swfinstitute.org/profiles/asset-manager
Published by the Sovereign Wealth Fund Institute (SWFI) with almost 3,300 shown. Shown here as there some cross-over with Hedge Funds.

PFX NOTE

 All the investor types mentioned in this chapter are registered as PFX Financiers. Rather than you spending time searching for them, they come to you by responding to your PFX listed Elevator Pitch and then, if they are interested, your Executive Summary.

PFX will act as the introducing intermediary but, after you have engaged with the investor, we step back so that you can take the transaction forward working directly with the investor.

CHAPTER 8:

FIFTEEN WAYS TO LOSE YOUR FUNDER

+

Way back in the olden days (1975), Paul Simon sung about *50 Ways to Lose Your Lover*. This will not make it into the charts, but here is our version: *15 Ways to Lose Your Funder*...

There are countless opportunities for you to alienate your funder, or even the gatekeeper who is going to open the door for you. You will have put in hundreds if not thousands of hours (the 'sweat equity') into your project planning, and probably spent hard cash.

So it would be tragic to see it all go south due to simple, and totally avoidable mistakes.

1. The executive summary looks like a sales brochure.

It is overflowing with information about how wonderful your project is going to be, but does not enable the funder to make a rapid yes/no decision if it fits their parameters.

Specifically, does it provide the answers to the 5W's + HM (Who, What, Where, When, Why + How Much) as presented in *Chapter 5: The Executive Summary and Submission*?

If this is not clearly presented right up front it is just another excuse for the funder to come back with the pre-programmed 'no' response. Remember, there are many other proposals in their inbox every morning!

2. You insist on the funder signing an NDA before sending your ES

Oh dear! Make no mistake, this is an instant deal breaker. Remember that funders and gatekeepers receive scores of unsolicited submissions weekly and, for larger firms, daily. What if they had to sign NDA and NCNDA on all of them first, before they could review each ES? This process would be time consuming as well as costly for financiers.

You need to accept that funders are in the business of financing projects, not stealing your IP.

3. E-mail overload.

You send the entire full deck for the project. The project plan, ES, drawings, permits, contracts, etc altogether attached to your e-mail, or several e-mails, thereby overwhelming the recipient and clogging up their inbox. The icing on this particular cake is not assigning proper file names to scanned documents, zipping them and leaving it to the funder and/or gatekeeper to unzip and open each file in turn to see what is in them.

The answer to all this is in *Chapter 5: The Executive Summary and Submission.*

4. Insisting on funder references.

This is understandable for those who have not yet caught up with the fact that most project financing now comes from private debt and equity sources.

A whole array of entities and new names have appeared in the market over the early 21st century, many of which were actually operating long before the 2008 banking crisis.

Private capital has made a permanent and tectonic impact on the global capital markets and that is the way it will stay for decades to come.

Private project finance providers must protect their proprietary programs as well as the identity of their investors and funded clients. Most funders will be happy to provide a letter from their lawyers confirming that they have the resource and expertise to actually provide the funding they are offering. That should suffice.

5. Grammatical and other errors in documents produced by project principals

Nothing looks worse than typing errors, misspelled names, unfinished spreadsheets, poor presentation etc. Run your spell check and make sure your documents are professionally prepared before sending them out and you should be fine.

6. Financials are incomplete, inconsistent or in the wrong currency

Precise and professionally prepared financials are naturally one of the key components of a successful project plan and submission. Only include the summary EBITDA for an appropriate time frame in your ES and show off the full details in your full spreadsheet, in its own folder in your Dropbox account or in-house data-room.

A common inhibitor to progress is that the financials have been produced completely in a local currency in which no-one will be prepared to fund.

Remember that you are entering a *global* market and that, if you are not working in EUR, GBP or USD, these are the currencies that most financiers expect the entire project to be presented as.

7. You categorically refuse to pay any fees whatsoever, except a success/completion fee

This must be one of the biggest obstacles across the project financing market. Principals take a stubborn stance against any kind of fee except their gatekeeper's or financiers structuring or other completion fee which is added to the loan amount.

Do not put pressure on your funder

If you tell the funder that your situation is urgent your

 application will be declined. No funder wants to be dragged into something where their analysts and other professionals are going to be driven by someone else's pressures.

Most investors charge a closing fee to cover their expenses on lawyers, due diligence, surveyor and other third party providers. This can sometimes be added to the loan.

The rationale for refusing to pay is usually that the principals have been 'burnt before' by paying upfront fees and provide elaborate examples. But this is never the whole story. A principal may have blindly paid an upfront fee to someone calling themselves a 'project financing advisor' who did nothing at the end of the day.

But the other explanation could be that the fee was paid to a gatekeeper, upon which they have reviewed the file and done their own DD on the project, and found fault in the submission. However, if this was the case, the client would have been advised and given every opportunity to put things right.

But the fact is that it costs actual, real money to prepare a project for financing. Professional fees covering accounting, legal, survey and other costs involved in structuring the financing cannot be avoided.

If you refuse to cover these costs you are asking the funder to cover the entire risk themselves and, naturally, they will not do it. As explained elsewhere in this book, you should expect fees anywhere between $25,000 (sometimes less) and $500,000 (sometimes more), depending on the complexity of your transaction.

8. Submitting a project based upon or containing fraudulent or misleading information

Whilst not prevalent, it happens more than one would think. Issues that principals can conceal include:

- Not disclosing pending or possible financial risks (lawsuit, divorce etc)
- Local community protests or objections against the project
- Past bankruptcies
- Debilitating or other serious medical conditions
- Shareholder disputes
- Existing loans

All the above, plus issues such as masked technical problems, convictions and more will all be exposed during the intense DD process. Any such revelation will bring the financing process to a close with the forfeiture of all fees paid thus far.

It is always best to be clear from the outset and let the gatekeeper, if there is one, and the funder in on any negative issues that might have an impact on the funding decision.

This will simply be taken into account in the project and risk evaluation and may not necessarily discourage the funder. For instance, many funders regard a past bankruptcy as a 'rite of passage' and a mark that the principal has learned many lessons the hard way.

9. You try to dictate the kind of funding structure or debt/equity ratios

Each funder will have their own structures in place, usually dictated by the mandate given them by their investors. If your PP insists on a specific structure, say you want 50% debt funding at 7% for ten years, and 50% equity then you are excluding all funders who do not meet these criteria.

Such insistence will give the funder the impression that you are not prepared to be flexible and that you could be disruptive and time consuming.

Today's project finance market is dictated by the financiers' current preferences which, in turn are dictated by those of their investors. Best to open your PP by saying that funding terms are negotiable.

10. You have no 'skin in the game'

In other words you have not invested any money into the project, and it is therefore a mere idea. This issue is covered elsewhere in this book under PFI (Project Finance Initiation) costs. The message here is quite simple, do not bring your project to market unless you can show you have spent real money on getting it to 'shovel ready' stage, and then have the reserve necessary to cover the cost of structuring your financing.

There is no 'free pass' into the project financing market.

11. The project is not submission ready

Permits, land, PPA's and all those other vital components are not in place. As explained in *Chapter 3: What is 'shovel ready'?*, funding is typically considered to be the last component part of any project.

If you are submitting your project and it is not ready to fund because this key documentation is missing, then your project is simply not 'shovel ready' and at a stage where it can be funded.

How would you expect a funder to invest in a solar farm if the permits are still missing? What assurances would there be that the project would actually get traction?

Make sure that you are *truly* shovel ready, otherwise you are wasting your own and the financier's time.

Also, it costs time (money) for the financier to review a submission and a poorly prepared or misleading one will not get a second chance.

12. You have spent all your money

It happens all the time. The principals have forgotten about allocating funds to the actual financing process. All these preliminary steps cost money, sometimes a lot of money, and now your funds are exhausted. It is as vital to budget your funds to cover funding transaction costs as it is to cover PFI because, without having those costs covered, your financing cannot move forward.

If you don't have those funds to hand, find some way which will allow you to raise them. If you have to borrow them, keep in mind that a funding offer will be made to you on the strength and validity of the information you have provided. If you have any doubts about that, do not risk borrowing against your own imperfect plans.

13. E-mail blasts

To send your pitch to countless people will only draw responses from joker-brokers. Serious gatekeepers and funders will spot spam a mile away and will simply delete your e-mail.

To attach the whole contents of your project plan to your spam is the ultimate kiss of death.

14. You exhibit 'brilliant engineer syndrome'

You are a brilliant engineer and you are now ready to take your waste-to-energy plant forward with innovative new, yet proven, technology. You are now talking directly with a financier and your project financing is gaining traction.

At this stage, let it go. There have been numerous instances of deals failing simply because the client has wanted to be kept involved and to 'help' through every wrinkle of the financial structuring. Sometimes, even wanting to change the way things are being done.

You are expert at what you do, and your financier trusts that you are up to doing the job. Trust your financier to be expert at what they do, and leave them alone to get on with it. You have years of experience at what you do, and they have years of experience on their side of the transaction.

Try to interfere in the process and you will call your own discretion and acumen into question and your file will be closed.

15. Asking for POF (Proof of Funds)
Your financier is providing funds to you under mandates given to them, in turn, by their investors which are, overwhelmingly, channels through which private capital is making its way into the market.

Unlike institutional funders where most people will recognise the names involved or can go to any number of websites to check them out private capital is, by its very nature, kept *private*.

It is impossible for any funder to provide POF in any form. Some will have websites that will show their past activity, although this by its very nature is also private. Or you can ask for a generic letter 'To whom it may concern' from their lawyers confirming that they have the ability, expertise and resources to finance projects.

PFX NOTE

 If you ask them to, your PFX RM will guide you throughout the discussion and negotiation process with your financier.

Most financiers are very keen to get deals done as they want to show good, solid returns to their investors. But they have established ways of working and doing things which your PFX RM will be well aware of.

CHAPTER 9:

ENGAGEMENT AND PROTOCOLS

+

f all goes well, and a financier has expressed their wish to engage with you, this is the last stage of your journey.

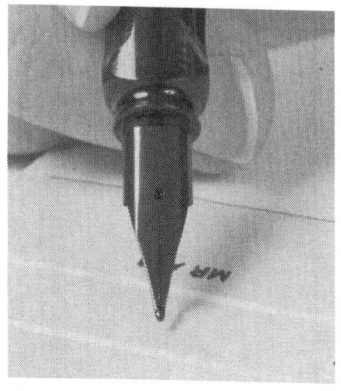

Provided all the information you have presented is complete, factual and unabridged you can be reasonably confident that, all things being equal, you are on the starting blocks to a successful financing.

Be prepared for a process that can take anywhere between 45 and 120 days and, depending on the nature and complexity of the deal, often longer. The pace of progress can sometimes seem glacial.

Usually the financier will provide you with an engagement agreement, which might include an NDA, and this may be exclusive or non-exclusive.

You are now dealing direct with a funder who could be handling dozens or scores of other projects at the same time. That is a lot of paper to review and financiers are averse to risking that kind of time and expenditure without any commitment from the client.

At the start of your dialogue with the funder it is important to clarify exactly what the legal, survey and other professional fees, which we describe as Project Finance Initiation (PFI), will be.

If they are beyond you, tell the financier as much at the outset so that nobody is wasting anybody's time.

It is important to understand that yours is not the only project in the world. Any financier meaning their analysts, underwriters and other professionals involved in your transaction, will warm to those clients who are responsive and diligent throughout the process.

Preconceptions

It is possible that you have someone on your team who has previously worked in banking or financial services. Or maybe, even, project finance. Or your accountant or lawyer may have had some involvement in previous project financings. Sometimes that can be an inhibitor rather than a benefit.

It is important to understand that your financier is, in turn, responsible to their own investors. These will overwhelmingly be U/HNWI's investing either directly or through their family office, hedge fund, private debt company or any one of a dozen other types of entities.

Consequently, each funder will have their own mandate given to them by their investors and, hence, each will have their own investment and lending preferences and structures.

The entity you are dealing with, even if it is a direct investor like a U/HNWI or their family office, is unique and they will have their own way of doing things.

So, if they are confronted with questions on their process and structure like 'Why don't you do it this way...?'; 'On my last deal we...'; 'Why can't you just fund the bank guarantee?'; 'Surely it would be better if...' or, the worst one of all, 'Who are your investors?' you will find your dialogue progressively closing down until there is nothing left to say.

Trust your funder
This one happens all the time and is one of the most frustrating aspects of the job for financiers. The project principals are all experts at their jobs. The lead engineer, the marketing and financial directors have all shown the track records on the PP that, along with all the other documentation, have given the financier the comfort they need to move forward. And then the micro-manager steps in.

I've never heard of you. Why should I be talking to you?

A perennial problem for project financiers in today's market is those project principals who come from a traditional banking background simply assuming that, because they have never heard of the funder, they are not up to the job.

But big name, traditional sources (banks) have largely withdrawn from the market and those that remain act as syndicators or aggregators rather than direct lenders.

Every step of the way the investor is challenged on every move they make, usually by the technical or engineering leader on the project team. They want to 'help' and ask questions about all aspects of the structure. On occasion, questions asked on intake and other forms are simply not answered because *they* do not think they are relevant.

From the get-go the investor needs to be left alone to get on with the job of financing, while you get on with yours. Trust them that they know what they are doing in the same way that they are trusting you to make the project work once your financing is in place.

Financing your project takes as many years of experience and education that your own project principals have in their specialities. It is never a straightforward process.

Terms sheet and completion

Once preliminary DD has been undertaken your financier may issue a non-binding terms sheet, LOI or some other preliminary commitment to the transaction. This will contain their full requirements to complete the funding process and will give indicative interest rate along with the term, or tenor (length) of the funding agreement.

It may be that you need this to take to some of your counter-parties in order that they will move forward from MOU or LOI to completing necessary contracts and agreements.

Usually the final, binding term sheet does not differ that much to the non-binding version. Except that it should say that all the requirements of the previous version have been met, and that to produce your actual loan agreement, which is usually where closing costs are incurred, all that is required is your signature on the document. It is at this stage that closing (third party) costs are usually expected to be paid.

> *"The pace of progress can*
>
> *sometimes seem glacial."*

Although your closing costs may be payable to lawyers, surveyors and other advisors it is usually the case that they are paid direct to the financier, rather than direct to the advisors, so that they can be absolutely sure that all fees have been paid to the right people and they are not going to hit a 'non-payment wall' at the closing stages.

Also there may be regulatory requirements, subject to the jurisdiction, where the funder is responsible for ensuring all such payments and engagements are valid and legitimate. This can be a complex area for the financier and, again, it is best simply to follow their lead.

Your loan agreement will then be produced within a matter of weeks. For the signing, depending on the location of both parties and how far apart they are, this can be done either through each party's nominees over a desk, or directly.

But, in whichever way, ink on paper is the norm.

Completion and closing

There are countless ways funds can be delivered into the SPV and whether it is released in tranches, on sight of architects or other EPC certificates or at various stages of construction are all depending on the financier's structure. Some want confirmation of each stage of construction before releasing the next tranche, others release funds *en bloc* to the client's account and others have their own way of doing things.

Once the loan agreement is signed, your funding will be assembled by the financier from their various investor sources before being released into your SPV. How long it takes for these funds to be assembled will depend entirely on where they are held by your financier's investors.

Or, if you are dealing with a PE, private debt, asset manager or similar firm with the necessary structure in place, they will be almost immediately (up to 30 days) available.

Remember, in many cases your funder is not sitting directly on a mountain of money, they have to draw down the funds for your project from their investors, who do not object provided your funder has met their mandates.

PFX NOTE

 At the critical closing stages of our deal PFX is happy to provide all the assistance you need. There are often questions raised by client's lawyers as to the financing structure, SPV, insurance Wraps and other matters, so it is essential you keep them informed at all stages.

The key to a smooth closing is transparency and information sharing throughout the entire transaction. Keep your lawyer or any other key parties involved all the way through.

Chapter 10:

Arbitrage Trading

There has been much written and said about arbitrage trading. Because of the opaqueness of the market it has been infested with opportunist fraudsters playing on the lack of knowledge about instruments such as SBLC's and BG's but, especially Swift MT's. Please see the Glossary at the end of this book for further information.

Arbitrage trading was first introduced by John Maynard Keynes, as private placement programs (PPP's) at the iconic Bretton Woods conference in 1944.

Then, it was structured to 'create' vast amounts of money to fund the rebuilding of devastated infrastructure after World War II. It required significant cash placements of $100 million or more which was usually provided by governments and major corporations. It was and still is a market for 'grown ups' where trust and personal relationships are more important than the transactions and documentation behind them.

Back then, everything was done on the phone and telex, with documentation carried all over the world by messengers. Over the subsequent eight decades it has evolved significantly with vast volumes of trades now carried out on-screen and with most documentation handled electronically.

But the principal is the same now, as it was back then. But instead of a few trades each week on large sums on small margins over many months, technology and rapidly advancing algorithms now facilitate huge volumes of smaller trades over just a few weeks.

The result is that placements can now be as small as $1m, but traders much prefer minimum deposits of $10 million in order to deliver really good results.

At the time of writing, there is a UK global A+-rated institution, one of the world's largest banks, offering a

40% per week return on minimum $10m placement. Funds remain in the investor's account, blocked by a Swift MT799. Meaning the funds cannot be used for any other purpose while the trades are in progress.

A U.S.-based global A+-rated bank is offering a monthly 100% return on placements of $1 million, with an escrow-type protection of funds managed by a leading US law firm.

That is how far the arbitrage trading process has advanced, to the distinct benefit of project principals, and investors. Depending on what level of funds can be placed into a program, equity in the project can be significantly enhanced, meaning debt funding will be much easier to secure. For investors, funds can remain in their account while the traders enhance their investable capital balance.

It is important to understand that to enter the market you need to be invited into it. Those are the regulations and the experience is far removed from that of mainstream banking or corporate finance.

Due diligence and AML

The market itself is unregulated but it is overseen by global institutions, including the IMF and other bodies, principally to ensure that it is not used for money laundering.

Anti-money laundering (AML) processes are constantly evolving with many checks on the identity of the client and their banks at every stage of the intake process.

For instance, you will expect to be asked for your bank manager's contact details. But to enter a trade you will need to provide a copy of their business card and sometimes with their signature over it. Also, the traders will not call them on the number on the business card, but go through the bank branch's main switchboard, to be absolutely sure they are really at the bank they say they are. Finally, they will be asked for their banker's PIN.

All this information is required by the trader's own bank, so that they know they are dealing with a genuine banking colleague when they contact them to set up the MT799, or whatever other instrument they are going to use to block your placement funds in your account while trades are ongoing.

Proof of Funds (POF)

The traders cannot use their own funds for the trades for all the obvious (hopefully) reasons. In order to protect your funds, they leave them in your account, usually using a Swift MT799 as the 'blocking' instrument, but arrange a loan against your funds which they use to start your trading cycle.

As part of your intake process you will need to add a screengrab of your current bank balance to the trader's KYC form. When the form is submitted the screengrab needs to be no more than three days old. No trader will countenance your submission if this POF (Proof of Funds) is not included in your KYC.

Proof of Life (POL)

A more recent AML process has been the introduction of the Proof of Life (POL) call.

This is where the trader will set up a video-call with the you to confirm you really are who you say you are. You will need to hold up a copy of a national newspaper purchased on the date of the call with the date on the front of the newspaper highlighted.

You will also need to hold up your passport, which you will also have copied into your KYC.

When this call is completed, your trades will be set up and usually commence within a week or two after that.

When POL was first introduced, the traders were happy simply with an image as presented below. However, there has been a more recent move towards video-calls, which are recorded.

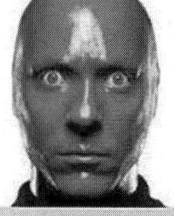

CURRENT
DATE
ENCIRLCEW/
RED LINE

FACE OF
SELLER/OWNER

BOND/CURRENCY/BOX+PASSPORT+
NEWSPAPER W. CLEAR LEGIBLE DATE

All this is in pursuance of the new Proof of Life requirements over and above the normal Proof of Funds and other requirements.

Profits

The proceeds from your trades, the profits, are not a loan of any sort. They have to be regarded and accounted for as profits into your business.

How much you benefit from your trades is directly relevant to how much you can place into them. If you are fortunate enough to be able to place a minimum $10 million into a trading cycle you will be able to fund a $250m project within a year to 18 months.

Obviously a smaller placement will deliver smaller returns.

For further information on arbitrage trading, please visit the 'Trade Desk' zone at the PFX website.

PFX NOTE

 PFX has introduced its Trade Desk, working with a highly reputable trade group, to ensure that clients are dealing only with real trades.

We have taken all steps to ensure that whatever program we put to you, your funds are never at risk. We will assist and guide clients along the way to a successful trade.

It is important to note that, once you have raised your full project financing, you can continue your trades, which must show as profits in your accounting.

CHAPTER 11:

PROJECT FINANCE EXCHANGE (PFX)
USER GUIDE

PFX has been launched to consolidate the $multi-trillion project finance market, bearing all the attributes of a global capital market in its own right.

It releases the flow of information, so that the flow of capital can naturally follow. This is the principle on which every stock, commodity or other exchange in the world operates.

INTRODUCTION

The market is comprised of an entire lexicon of channels through which private capital seeks to derive long-term, stable and, as far as possible, risk-free returns. These channels include:

Alternative investment managers | Asset managers | Single- and multi-family offices | Private debt and equity funds | Hedge funds | Private banks | Wealth managers

...and others totalling tens of thousands of private capital funds of all descriptions. They have total availability of private capital of many trillions of dollars ('dry powder'). More recently, some jurisdictions are enabling their regulated funds (pension, fixed-income, mutual etc) to participate in the market. Encouraged by the introduction of A+-rated insurance wraps.

In project finance transactions, investment analysts focus on the track record and financial stability of whoever is going to buy the output from the built project. In the case of a senior living facility, the investor will look for agreements with insurance companies or sovereign underwriting, depending on the jurisdiction.

In the case of a waste-to-energy plant, the focus will be on whoever is going to buy the electricity it produces. Be that a grid, car plant or anything else. The proposers will obviously need to show business acumen and market experience, but their assets and balance sheet come second to the buyer of the plant's output.

RAISING PROJECT FINANCE THROUGH PFX

A senior living project will require confirmation of insurance or sovereign guarantees for residential care.

To raise finance through PFX it is simply a matter of going to the 'Submit Project' zone at the PFX website at www.projectfinanceexchange.com. From there you can download the Intake Form and Listings Worksheet.

Intake Form

This asks for details of your company and other KYC (Know Your Client) information. It then asks a list of questions regarding every aspect of your project from deal value, through market sector, permits and permissions secured to off-take agreements. This enables PFX analysts to assess if your project is fully 'submission ready', or still in need of work to bring it up to the standards investors require.

Very few submissions meet PFX and its investors' submission ready standards. Depending on how much additional work is required a decision will be made whether to invest the time needed to bring it up to standard, or if time will have to be charged for. PFX absolutely recommends that, if the skills are not available in-house, money is spent on getting the submission right first time with the help of a consultant. But it is important to ensure that they demonstrate actual experience in producing a submission ready *project* plan, as opposed to a traditional business plan.

Listings Worksheet

This has broken down the component parts of the Executive Summary under various headings. Usually your PFX Regional Manager or analyst will lift all the relevant information out of your ES and/or project plan to populate the fields shown. But you can lighten the load by doing it yourself and leaving it to PFX to edit. Once completed, the content is then cut and pasted into the relevant fields on the PFX dashboard, from where it appears on the listings at the site.

From there the Elevator Pitch (EP), which appears on the site listings is sent to PFX online registered investors whose pre-set preferences your deal matches. If they like the look of the EP, they can then click through to the full ES (only available to registered investors) and contact the PFX RM or analyst handling the transaction.

Alternatively, for larger deals, the PFX Concierge will identify specific investors who will be interested in your project, based on their preferences and past experience of their activities.

Once an investor has agreed to move forward with your transaction PFX steps back, but remains available to provide support and input wherever it is needed.

Fees

Online registered investors: You will have a fee agreement with your RM which will be presented in their engagement agreement with you.

Concierge investors: PFX will have a direct fee agreement with the investor, and there is no fee charged to you.

Investors can view PFX as complementary to their existing deal origination processes.

You can regard PFX a being entirely complementary to your existing deal original processes. Although you will find it far more time-and cost-effective than what you are already doing.

With thousands of financiers and as many thousands of projects around the world, to say that our market is fragmented would be an understatement. You already know about the inefficiencies and costs this inflicts on our market.

PFX is the only informed and structured solution designed to overcome this frustrating *status quo*. We bring fintech to project finance but, to ensure quality control, with the essential human touch through our PFX Regional Managers.

As a genuine project financier there is no charge to register.

- All financing submissions presented in a consistent, standard format designed to meet the demands of any project financier. We recommend you assign one person in you organisation to manage your PFX account.

- Set your preferences and await the arrival of elevator pitches (takes just a minute to read) for deals that match your requirements, and includes indicators as to their state of 'shovel readiness'.

Request and review executive summaries before deciding to engage. The PFX Regional Manager will discuss the deal with you. They can move forward with just ONE investor at a time, ensuring that you are not being 'played off' against others.

Online registration
This is for smaller (sub-$1bn) funds with a local, regional or national remit. There is no charge to register. From the 'Investors' zone just follow the navigation and confirm your e-mail address. Once this is done it is simply a matter of logging back in, setting your preferences and submitting your registration.

All investor registrations go through the PFX due diligence process which filters out the many frauds that prevail across the market. From hard experience, and using systems and processes that are unique to PFX, many advance fee fraudsters attempting to register with PFX have been, and continue to be declined.

Concierge service

This service was introduced after it became clear that larger, global investors usually with $1bn investable capital or more, wanted a more personal service. You can contact the Concierge through the 'Investors' zone at the PFX site and he will contact you directly.

He will discuss your specific investment preferences with you and then monitor and navigate PFX for you. He will then notify you of (usually larger) deals that match your interests.

Unlike the online registration service, PFX will contact with you directly, using your intermediary/introducer template and agree the fee schedule with you.

PFX Regional Managers

PFX is approached regularly by intermediaries, consultants and professionals of all descriptions to become PFX Regional Managers. But the fact is that project finance is a highly specialist professional discipline that can only be learned through actual participation in the market, often learning many painful and expensive lessons along the way.

PFX constantly promotes the message that academia, worldwide, is still teaching the project finance structure as if nothing has changed since it was first developed back in the 1950's for the financing of large scale industrial and infrastructure projects by leading, global institutions.

If you can demonstrate a solid track record of successful project finance transactions, have a current pipeline of submission ready projects and are prepared to adapt your existing processes to PFX's proven fintech, we want to hear from you.

For further information, please go to the 'Work With Us' zone at the PFX website.

PFX Associates provide quality control

PFX has brought fintech to project finance, built on the long-accepted protocols and processes of this global market. But fintech alone can never replace the essential human involvement and relationships on which this market depends.

There is still a need for quality control of project submissions before the financier gets to see them, and our PFX Regional Managers (RM) are front and centre of that quality control.

No-one can post their own deal to PFX. Your role, as a PFX RM is to ensure the essential quality control that PFX investors demand. We seek only the cream. Seasoned, experienced and methodical project finance intermediaries. Those who understand that each project and the people behind it are unique, that transactions cannot be rushed and that there are no 'fast bucks' to be made. If this is you, and you can meet our registration criteria, we will welcome you as a PFX RM. Our registration process is designed to eliminate 'joker brokers'.

This Guide has been prepared to walk you through the processes built into PFX, which are all based on long-established market protocols with which, if you have the experience, you will be familiar.

Registration

Each application for registration as a PFX RM is reviewed individually. We look at your website (and/or LinkedIn profile) and search the web to see if there are any adverse reviews of you or your organisation.

Fees

There are two separate fee structures based on points on final funded amount:

Online registered investors: You will have a PFX template engagement agreement with your client which provides for fee payment direct to you from the client on completion on the following scale:

Sub-10m to 250:	3%
250m to 500m:	2.5%
500m to 1bn:	2%
1bn+:	1%

Concierge investors: PFX will have a fee agreement directly with the investor, in which case you will receive 40% of the fee paid to PFX by the investor.

Key Stage Roles

Assist in preparing the project for listing on PFX

Your key stage roles as a PFX Associate are as follows:

1. Review the project's documentation ensuring
    that all those originated by the project itself
    (project plan, financials, cv's etc) are of an
    acceptable standard for 'readability' and content.
    Also all (where appropriate) permits, permissions,
    EPC, offtake, feedstock, operating, land, access
    and other essential contracts, agreements and
    other documentation is available to the financier.

2. Through your dashboard create an Intake Form
    for your client and allocate them a six-digit
    Project Indicator (PI) code. Content from the
    Intake Form is also used to create the Executive
    Summary which is sent in response to enquiries
    from potential Financiers.

3. Create a shortform company name for the client
    for use in your Engagement Agreement.
    ⓘ Ie: Alliance Energy Partners will become 'AEP' or
    'Alliance' throughout the Agreement.

4. Click the 'Create Engagement Agreement' button
    on your Dashboard. This will automatically create
    the agreement as a .pdf ready for your and the
    client's signature.

5. Assess the client's financial resource and to what level their ability to meet financier's DD/closing costs are.

6. Assist in preparing the project's submission for posting to PFX.

7. Ensure that all documentation is presented in Dropbox or other data-room in accordance with guidance set out in *The RAISING PROJECT FINANCE Handbook* (the Handbook).

8. Review the client's elevator pitch for all content and, most importantly, *no client contact information* appearing in the 250-word summary.
   The elevator pitch is built by PFX using data provided on the client's Intake Form and sent to PFX financiers according to their pre-set preferences of deal-value, location, market sector and other criteria. It also appears on the screen when any visitor to PFX clicks on a listing by scrolling through the home page while browsing all or selecting by region, market sector and deal value).

9. Prepare and upload to the client's account (managed from your dashboard) the executive summary which is part-prepared from the Intake

Form. It must not include any contact information for either yourself or your client.

Financiers receive the ES if they click 'Request Executive Summary' on the elevator pitch. No client contact information can appear in order to avoid possible circumvention. If financiers want to move forward, they click 'Engage' on the ES and you are notified of their interest through your dashboard which provides the following information:

Contact Name | company | website |e-mail | phone | country | financier type | year established | closing cost range | languages spoken.

*You can call each financier you think it worthwhile talking to in order to get an understanding of how they operate and to assess if you feel the client will be able to work with them. Much of the conversation will centre on the client's stage of 'shovel readiness'. However, you can only click the 'Engage' button against **just one** financier. Once you have clicked 'engage' all other enquiries are advised that they are 'declined'. This reassures your chosen financier* *that they are not being 'played off' against others.*

10. Ensure that *all file names* across Dropbox are prefixed with the six-digit Project Indicator (PI) code you allocated to the project.

    ⓘ This provides a 'tracking' mechanism for the client, you and the financiers when they are sharing client files between analysts, underwriters and others involved in their financing structure.

11. Execute posting of the project to PFX.

12. After you have received enquiries over a period of ten working days, discuss the project (no identity disclosures) with those you feel are the best for your client to work with. Once decided, click the appropriate 'Engage' button.

    ⓘ You may engage with just one financier from those presented, which is to reassure financiers that they are not being 'played off' against others.

13. Provide support to the client throughout the negotiation process.

14. Advise PFX when a completion date and final financing amount across all structures has been issued by the financier.

Posting the project to PFX

The following checklist broadly outlines the posting process which you carry out through your dashboard:

- Confirm elevator pitch reviewed (no contact details to show)
- Confirm Project Plan is prepared in accordance with guidance in
  Chapter 4 of *The RAISING PROJECT FINANCE Handbook*

- Confirm Dropbox/data-room content as described in *The RAISING PROJECT FINANCE Handbook* reviewed

- Confirm Executive Summary *with no contact details* uploaded

PFX actions on listing:

- The headline from the project elevator pitch along with the deal value, market sector and country is added to the PFX Pipeline listings on the home page (where all visitors can view) and click to view Elevator Pitch.
- Elevator Pitch sent to all financiers whose pre-set preferences it matches.

- Each elevator pitch can be shared on LinkedIn, Facebook and Twitter.
- Financiers can respond to the Elevator Pitch by clicking 'Request Executive Summary', which provides the ES you have prepared.
- If they wish to move forward, they can click 'Engage' on the ES which triggers an alert on your dashboard and adds the Financier to the client file.

Reviewing financier enquiries:

The structure presented below is designed to assure financiers that when they engage with the client through PFX they are not unknowingly being 'played off' against other financiers.

Alongside each financier shown on your dashboard there are two buttons 'Engage' and 'Decline'. When you click 'Engage' against your preferred financier:

- All other financiers are automatically advised that the project has now engaged with their preferred financier.
- Full contact details of the financier are sent to the client. They are advised not to contact them until YOU have arranged the initial conference call.
- The project is suspended from the PFX listings. Greyed out with a 'Transaction in Progress' banner.
- The financier is sent full contact details and KYC information of the project and yourself together

with their Dropbox or data room link. They are advised that you will be in touch after three working days to arrange a conference call with the client (to allow them time to review all documentation).

Failed Transactions

If negotiations fail for any of the countless reasons of which you will be aware, you can restore the project to the PFX listings at no additional cost.

GLOSSARY

AUM. Assets Under Management.

Used to describe the amount of capital or physical assets managed by a Hedge Fund, Asset Manager or similar entity.

Arbitrage.

The simultaneous purchase and sale of the same or similar asset in different markets in order to profit from tiny differences in the listed price. It exploits short-lived variations in the price of identical or similar financial instruments in different markets or in different forms.

Originally developed by John Maynard Keynes and presented at the Bretton Woods conference in 1944, it has since evolved to become far more widely available. Cash placements to enter programs have reduced from $100m to $1m since the around 2010 onwards.

BG (Bank Guarantee).

A 'promise' to make payment to a third party under certain circumstances – such as the failure of obligations from the buyer.

DD. Due diligence.

Where the funder reviews and checks all your documentation, validates and verifies all the information you have provided on your company and its shareholders and directors and otherwise assures themselves that they are lending to/investing in a genuine project on behalf of their own investors or other capital sources. As the client, you are of course entitled to undertake your own DD on the lender if they are not a familiar name.

Origination

The term used by investors to describe executives tasked with the responsibility to identify new project finance transactions that meet their financing criteria.

ES. Executive Summary.

A summarised version of the full Project Plan designed to present all key aspects of the project to an intake or origination executive.

EBITDA. Earnings Before Interest, Tax, Depreciation and Amortization.

Gross earnings with nothing taken out.

EPC. Engineering and Procurement Contractor.

The company that will manage the entire build of your project, possibly working with a separate project manager with experience specific to your own project.

Family Office (Single or Multiple)

A single family office is an entity through which a wealthy family manage their financial affairs including tax, investment, legacy, succession and other matters. A multi-family offices manages these affairs for a number of client families. Members of these families are usually U/HNWI's in their own right.

Gatekeeper or Intermediary

A project financing advisor who works directly with their funding sources and is paid an introducer fee directly by the funder. They therefore do not require a completion fee from the project principals. *Note: No fee agreement should be signed with any advisor without sight of confirmation that the funder is in agreement with that fee agreement.*

HOA. Heads of Agreement.
The same as HOT. High level terms under which two parties are ready to move towards a final agreement.

HOT. Heads of Terms.
The same as HOA. High level terms under which two parties are ready to move towards a final agreement.

IP. Intellectual Property.
Defined by WIPO (World Intellectual Property Organisation) as creations of the mind, such as inventions; literary and artistic works; designs; and symbols, names and images used in commerce.

IPO. Initial Public Offering.
Taking a company from private to public ownership through a listing on a stock exchange.

IWPF. Insurance Wrapped Project Finance.
A process that endows qualifying projects to be assigned the Lloyds of London insurance market 'A' credit agency rating enabling the release of institutional funding into them. Funds are provided as 100% debt on the same or similar terms as those enjoyed by municipalities, major corporations and other 'A' rated entities.

LTV. Loan to Value.
Describes the proportion of the total asset value the lender is expecting the borrower to contribute. An LTV of 10% on a $100 million transaction means the lender is expecting a contribution of $10 million from the borrower.

LVR. Loan to Value Ratio.

The ratio of the loan to the finished value of the project. So an LVR of 50% on a hotel project with a finished, built value of $200 million would be the $100 million construction cost.

MOU. Memorandum of Understanding.

A document between the project principals and a supplier, contractor or off-taker presenting the terms under which both are prepared to move towards a firm contract.

MT (Message Type)

A system of inter-bank/institutional messaging which can be applied to specific financial transactions. It is operated by the global Swift banking network (see below). The full list can be found by searching: 'swift message types'.

NDA. Non-Disclosure Agreement.

An agreement between parties to an agreement that nothing within that agreement or coming out of it will be disclosed to anyone outside of it.

NCNDA. Non-Circumvention and Non-Disclosure Agreement.

The same as an NDA except that the parties also agree not to go around anyone who is party to the agreement or the transaction it covers to a third party introduced to the transaction by a party to the NCNDA.

O&G. Oil & Gas.

Self explanatory.

O&M Contract

Operations & Management Contract, usually associated with a construction which needs ongoing maintenance such as a renewable energy plant.

OMA. Operations & Management Agreement.
The agreement with the company that will manage the hotel, airport, hospital or other property being developed and from which revenues paid will repay the project financing.

Operating EBITDA
EBITDA from the point the built project starts operating and generating revenues. This can sometimes be referred to as post-stabilisation EBITDA, but project financiers need to see it from the moment the project starts operating to when it stabilises, which can take up to five years (sometimes longer).

PFI. Project Finance Initiation.
Costs incurred in bringing the project to a stage where it will be considered 'shovel ready' by a financier.

PPA. Power Purchase Agreement.
The agreement between a project that will generate power (renewable or otherwise) and a power distribution network, grid or company.

PPP. Private Placement Program.
An unregulated *private* market that accelerates returns on a blocked *placement* of funds (usually €50m+). Returns from a PPP are 'profit' as opposed to 'interest'. Often used to provide funds, which are not repaid, for major projects with those funds consumed by labour and materials thus leaving no effect on inflation.

PP. Project Plan.
The full, comprehensive and detailed presentation of the project in its entirety. Contains all contracts, background, financials and other information that a financier will need to assess its viability and suitability to their funding structure (s).

RE. Real Estate.
Covers a multitude of construction projects from residential and commercial through to hotels and hospitals.

SBLC. Standy Letter of Credit
A legal instrument issued by a bank on behalf of its client, providing a guarantee of its commitment to pay the seller if its client (the buyer) defaults on the agreement.

Shovel Ready.
The stage of development of a project where the only outstanding matter to be resolved is *only* the financing itself. Only the investor and their counterparties can declare a project to be 'shovel ready'.

SPV. Special Purpose Vehicle.
A company or other entity established specifically for the funding, construction and operation of the project.

SWIFT. Société for Worldwide Interbank Financial Telecommunications.
A global network set up by the banking industry through which financial transactions by banks and other institutions can initiate and execute transactions specific to their needs. It uses a system of MT's (Message Types) which can be applied to specific needs.

U/HWNI. Ultra- and High-Net Worth Individual.
Depending on who is doing the definitions, a HNWI is someone with a minimum $1 million liquid cash over and above all personal assets and liabilities. UHNWI's are defined as having anywhere between $250 and $500 million disposable up to and beyond $1 billion.

W2E.   Waste-to-Energy. (sometimes 'Energy from Waste')

A process that converts waste (mostly municipal) to energy, sometimes along with other by-products such as bio-diesel.

Thank you for reading

The RAISING PROJECT FINANCE Handbook

The Official

User Guide

If you found this book helpful please be sure to give it your full 5-star rating on Amazon! Thank you.